YANKEES

Where Have You Gone?

BY
MAURY ALLEN

WWW.SPORTSPUBLISHINGLLC.COM

Director of production: Susan M. Moyer
Book design: Jennifer Polson
Developmental editor: Doug Hoepker
Project manager: Greg Hickman
Dust jacket design: Kenneth J. O'Brien
Card design: Christine Mohrbacher
Copy editor: Holly Birch
Cover photo: Mark Jones
Interior photos: Brace Photo, unless otherwise noted
Insert photos: Courtesy of individuals photographed

ISBN: 1-58261-719-8

Printed in the United States.

For Janet

My wife, my pal, my partner, in all things personal and professional, with total love and affection, devotion and dedication, joy and emotion for all the years past, present and future.

CONTENTS

INTRODUCTION

In 101 seasons in New York and 81 years at the Stadium, the New York Yankees have recorded 26 World Series titles and 39 first-place finishes.

They have become the standard of excellence in sports, outdistancing every other team in baseball by far with titles and standing high above any other sports franchise.

They have played before a billion people in person at the Stadium or on the road and been seen by tens of billions on television.

Their *NY* logo is the most valuable in sports. Fans can be seen wearing Yankee baseball caps from the Bronx to the Bahamas, from Manhattan to Malaysia, from Staten Island to Saudi Arabia.

Many American soldiers from Kosovo to Kuwait switch from military helmets to Yankee caps in their moments of relaxation.

Former New York City mayor Rudy Giuliani can be spotted wearing his Yankee cap while sitting on the American League bench at the All-Star game in Milwaukee, and comedian Billy Crystal wears his cap in love scenes from *When Harry Met Sally.*

Military commander Tommy Franks, on a Stadium visit with owner George Steinbrenner, was asked if he was a Yankee fan. "Isn't everybody?" the general asked.

"Never bet against the Yankees, Notre Dame or General Motors," became a standard description of the sure things in sports and business in American life.

The fame of the team has cut across every segment of American life—from brain surgeons and rocket scientists to plumbers and ditch diggers. From persons of every race, religion and ethnic background, from every geographic center in the United States and around the world—if Americans show up, the New York Yankees are there.

It all started slowly when a bad team from Baltimore moved to New York in 1903. It grew into a frenzy with the arrival of Babe Ruth on the Yankee scene in 1920 at the Polo Grounds, a home field shared with the New York Giants. By 1923, The House That Ruth Built was open and christened with a Ruth homer on opening day.

Soon, a youngster from the New York streets named Henry Louis Gehrig would join the team and help lead the 1927 Yankees, maybe the best club the game has ever seen, into legendary status.

Joe DiMaggio brought his quiet aura to the Yankees in 1936. A fleet of feet rookie named Mickey Charles Mantle would team with DiMaggio for a single season in 1951.

Mantle, the handsome blond kid from Commerce, Oklahoma, grew into the team's anchor star for the next decade as the most powerful switch hitter the game had ever seen.

Roger Maris would break the legendary Ruth home run mark in 1961 with 61 homers, a feat no asterisk could possibly diminish.

Hall of Famers Bill Dickey, Whitey Ford, Yogi Berra, Phil Rizzuto, Catfish Hunter, Reggie Jackson, Dave Winfield—some 41 in all—would bring gold and glory to the Yankee scene in the 20th century.

All these glorious players became legendary figures, high-priced collectibles at card shows, names repeated in baseball tales over a generation.

But what of the other 2,500 players who wore Yankee uniforms, shared games and dinners with the stars, put in some difficult years, maybe never even won a pennant or earned a World Series ring?

Each in his own way added to the team's history, legends, and memories of Yankee accomplishments of the past.

Now it is time to recognize and appreciate them. It is in this work that we salute some 50 representatives of all the Yankee players of the past. We want to know them better, to appreciate them more, to honor them for their own individual contributions to the Yankee legend.

"Where Have You Gone, Joe DiMaggio?" wrote Paul Simon and Art Garfunkel in their classic song "Mrs. Robinson." Where *have* they all gone? What happened to them? Whatever happened to Dooley Womack?

DOOLEY WOMACK

He was a winning pitcher at 7-3 on the only 10th place Yankee finishers of all time, the 1966 New York Yankees who ended the season a mere 26.5 games out of first place as the CBS-owned team bottomed out.

His name was Dooley Womack, enough of a reason for a smile, and his teammates included legendary Mickey Mantle, home run king Roger Maris and excellent writer Jim Bouton.

Horace Guy Womack of Columbia, South Carolina was a right-handed relief pitcher with a high voice, a serious drawl and a giddy laugh. He won 19 big-league games in five seasons, and then he went back home to Weeping Cherry Lane in Columbia.

"When I went to spring training my locker was right next to the door," he recalled. "I knew they could throw my stuff out at any time."

Manager Johnny Keane pitched him often that spring, and catcher Jake Gibbs, a fellow southerner from Mississippi, reminded him that he could make the club. He faced the Atlanta Braves a few days before the Yankees broke camp and he retired Joe Torre, Henry Aaron and Rico Carty, three of the game's best hitters, in order.

SEASONS WITH YANKEES: 1966-68

Best Season with Yankees: 1967

Games: 65 (fourth in AL) • **Record: 5-6** • Saves: 18 (fourth in AL) • **ERA: 2.41** • Innings Pitched: 97 • **Hits Allowed: 80** • Strikeouts: 57 • **Walks: 35**

"I was flying 10 feet high when we got on the plane to fly north for the season," Womack said. "Then the captain made an announcement that the plane was returning to the gate. I told Jake it was because they were sending me back to the minors."

Instead he became a Yankee in New York, pitched in 42 games, recorded an impressive 2.64 ERA and became a fan favorite because of his smile and his style.

"That first day in the Stadium I just walked on the field in street clothes and looked all around. I was in the House That Ruth Built, I was a Yankee, I was in the big leagues, in New York City," he said.

As a youngster he had acquired the nickname of Dooley from a family friend who was called Dool. He was soon Dooley to family and friends and Horace in his classrooms in school.

"Horace was always a guy standing on a corner with a tie, a suit and a briefcase. That wasn't me. I was always with a ball and a bat," he said.

He was signed by the Yankees after pitching in one of his worst amateur games, a 15-13 win.

"I think they just wanted to see if I would hang in there when things went bad. I sure did," he said.

Womack was given a $2,500 bonus by the Yankees and it became a standard joke when he joined the team in 1966. Mickey Mantle had only been given a $500 bonus before he started his Hall of Fame career.

"I used to say to Mickey that he would have gotten more money if he had better legs," said Womack. "Mickey would always laugh and say if he had better legs he wouldn't be here."

While the Yankees struggled that season and GM Ralph Houk replaced Keane as manager, Womack became more comfortable with his role on the Yankees.

"[Yankee coach] Wally Moses helped me with a pitch, and I started feeling more confident that I could get big-league hitters out. Frank Robinson [traded over from Cincinnati to Baltimore that year] said in the papers that I was the toughest guy he faced all year," Womack recalled.

His greatest thrill came when Mantle hit his 500th career homer against Baltimore in a game Womack won in relief.

"When we got into the clubhouse Mickey just came up to me and said, 'Thanks for letting me enjoy my 500th.' If we lost it would have been awful quiet," Womack said.

He had one more thrill with Mantle on the receiving end of it. In 1968, former Dodger catcher John Roseboro, playing with Minnesota, hit a wicked line drive off Womack's leg with runners on second and first and none out. Third baseman Bobby Cox touched third, threw to second for the second out and Horace Clarke fired to Mantle at first for a triple play.

Womack spent a couple more seasons with the Yankees and then finished up with Houston, Seattle and finally the Oakland A's in 1970.

"After I came home, a lot of guys kidded me by calling me a 'Damn Yankee.' They said I sounded like I came from New York. I probably picked up a few New York words while I was there," he said.

"I had to get a real job after that, and I got into the sale of men's clothing. I had pitched before 50,000 people and now I was trying to sell one guy a pair of pants. It was a little bit of a comedown," he said.

Womack tried real estate for a while, drifted into carpet sales and finally landed a sales position with a company that made commercial flooring. He spent 23 years with the company before retiring a couple of years ago.

At the age of 64 with two children and four grandchildren, he coaches American Legion teams, plays lots of golf, watches the game on television and gets excited when he receives an alumni magazine from the Yankees or gets a rare invitation to the Yankee Old Timers Day.

"I never had any souvenirs when I left the Yankees. We didn't do that in those days. A few years back they invited me to New York and sent me a uniform—number 58. I put it on and got nervous all over again. I thought I could still hear the crowds," he recalled.

Womack acknowledges that today's huge salaries certainly have changed the game, and he knows the modern players don't have as much fun on the planes and team buses as he had with Mantle, Maris, Bouton, Gibbs, Fritz Peterson and all the rest.

"How could they? They just sit there with their laptops and cell phones calling their agents, accountants and business managers," he said.

He still enjoys studying the pitchers on television and guessing about the next pitch.

"Pitching is a psychic event," he explains, "you against the hitter. It's all about who is best on one particular pitch."

Womack remembers his Yankee days with fondness and affection for the memories and his teammates. He has a bad back now, and the 30 years since he stopped playing haven't been very easy.

"I just remember it all as a wonderful experience, the biggest part of my life," he said. "There was this one time I had gone 12 games without giving up a run. Houk kidded me by saying I might get my butt kicked next time. That was the night. I was down. He just came over and said, 'There's always tomorrow.'"

In recent years he has been battling a bad back with three separate operations to deal with a disc problem.

"My son had the same thing. Maybe we inherited it. I don't know. My dad had a strong back and a weak mind. Now I got a weak back *and* a weak mind," he laughed.

They might call him a 'Damn Yankee' in Columbia. So what. It will just bring a lot of smiles to Dooley Womack's face.

PHIL LINZ

About 40 years ago Phil Linz played a few notes of "Mary Had A Little Lamb" on the cheap harmonica he bought the day before on the Yankee team bus.

It was a hot, sticky, uncomfortable day and the crowded school bus without air conditioning was taking the downcast Yankees from a loss in Chicago to O'Hare airport for their flight on to Boston.

Linz, a utility infielder playing shortstop in place of the injured Tony Kubek, got only a few sounds out before coach Frank Crosetti demanded he stop the music.

Linz asked teammate Mickey Mantle, sitting just behind him, what Crosetti had said.

Mantle, the legendary Yankee player and kidder, deadpanned to Linz, "He said to play louder."

Linz obeyed Mantle. Then rookie manager Yogi Berra stormed to the back of the bus from his front seat and demanded the harmonica. Linz flipped it to the skipper, and Yogi heaved it back toward Linz, hitting teammate Joe Pepitone on the knee. Pepitone howled in mock pain.

"I guess that's what most people know me for," said Linz.

SEASONS WITH YANKEES: 1962-65

Best Season with Yankees: 1964

Games: 112 • Batting Average: .250 • At Bats: 368 • Hits: 92 •
Runs: 63 • Home Runs 5 • RBI: 25

The next day Berra fined Linz $200. He could afford to pay, as he had recently signed a $10,000 contract to promote the harmonica with the company that made it.

In seven big-league seasons with the Yankees, Phillies and Mets, Linz batted .235 in 519 games. He was as well known for his quips as for his hits, including two World Series homers in 1964 against the St. Louis Cardinals, one of them off Hall of Famer Bob Gibson.

Linz loved being a Yankee even though he might have played more games with other teams. When trade rumors flew around the club one year he quipped, "Play me or keep me."

Linz was an outstanding amateur player around the Baltimore area, where he was born June 4, 1939, and made it to the Yankees in 1962 along with pals Pepitone and Jim Bouton. He played on Yankee pennant winners in his first three seasons before the team collapsed with age in the 1965 season under new manager Johnny Keane.

"I knew I wasn't going to be a regular on the Yankees. They had Tony Kubek and Bobby Richardson at short and second ahead of me, but it was good enough just to sit on the Yankee bench," he said.

He was tall and thin, standing six foot one and weighing about 180 pounds at his peak. He had an open stance and could drive the ball hard on occasion. He once hit a double off hard thrower Juan Pizarro that caused most of his teammates to faint on the bench.

"When I first came up I had an open stance like Joe DiMaggio. I thought I would be the next Joe DiMaggio. Then I got into a few games," he laughed.

In his first big-league game he faced a hard-throwing Kansas City righthander named Dan Pfister. He made outs his first two times up and then drove a ball over the left field wall for a home run in his third at-bat in the big leagues.

"I was pretty impressed with that," he said. "I guess Kansas City wasn't. They sent Pfister out to the minors the next day."

While he backed up Kubek and played infrequently, he became one of the most popular Yankees around. The team had a dour personality with explosions by Mantle or Roger Maris against the press after any losing effort. Linz was good for a laugh, win or lose.

In the last six weeks of the 1964 season, he was a key player as the Yankees rallied under Berra to win the pennant. The Cardinals beat them in a stirring seven-game Series with Linz homering off Gibson in the final game. He also homered in the second game, won by Yankee rookie pitcher Mel Stottlemyre.

Keane, managing the Cardinals before moving to New York for the next season, never wavered about removing Gibson even after the Yankees threatened in the ninth inning.

In one of baseball's most emotional lines, Keane explained why he didn't take the tiring Gibson out of the game.

"I had a commitment to his heart," Keane said of his pitcher.

Linz had a short stay in Philadelphia and ended up with the Mets. He finished his career in 1968 with an 0-for-25 batting streak, no threat to DiMaggio's 56-game streak.

While playing for the Mets, he opened up a restaurant and night spot on the east side of Manhattan called Mr. Laffs with partners Art Shamsky of the Mets and football Giants star Bob Anderson. The place was a hangout for stewardesses, athletes, young businessmen and bon vivants. It was packed almost every night with a lot of name-droppers making it into the local gossip columns.

"We had a real good run there in the 1960s and 1970s with the hippies and the swingers," he said. "Then everybody started staying late in their offices to make money, and we went out of business."

He later joined Shamsky in an employment business, got into insurance sales and eventually worked his way into real estate investment for a large Manhattan investment company.

Linz and his wife, Lyn, a former flight attendant, have one son, Philip, a waiter in a fashionable Manhattan eatery.

Linz often appears at baseball card shows, is a frequent guest at sports banquets and spends a great deal of time appearing at charity golf outings in the New York area. He makes his home in Stamford, Connecticut, where he helped coach his son's teams.

"I still get a lot of requests for my autograph and for appearances now, even after all these years out of the game. I guess the harmonica incident did it for me. I just loved every minute of playing," he said.

As for his relationship with his former manager Yogi Berra, later a coach on the Mets when Linz joined that team, they have been pals ever since the incident.

Linz has a business card from his investment company showing a picture of himself playing the harmonica while wearing his Mets uniform. The guy covering his ears with a big smile on his face is none other than Yogi Berra.

HANK BAUER

He was once described as having a face like a clenched fist.

Hank Bauer, who turned 81 on July 31, 2003, is still not a guy to fool with. He can bite your head off with a quick remark or intimidate you with a stare.

That's what most of his Yankee teammates remember him for.

"Don't fool with my money," he once bellowed to a young Mickey Mantle when Mantle failed to run out a ground ball.

Despite a long, tough battle with throat cancer that damaged his gruff voice, Bauer is still a presence at Yankee Old Timers days in New York. He is popular as a spring training visitor, at baseball card shows and banquets, at baseball fantasy camps and at many sports events in his hometown of Kansas City.

Bauer, the father of four and the grandfather of 12, makes his home in Shawnee Mission, Kansas where he fishes and hunts to his heart's content.

Henry Albert Bauer was born in East St. Louis, Illinois in a blue-collar community, played amateur baseball in the late 1930s and joined the Marines shortly after the outbreak of World War II. He saw combat in the South Pacific before coming back to baseball to join the Yankees in 1948.

hank bauer

YANKEES   OUTFIELD

SEASONS WITH YANKEES: 1948-59

Best Season with Yankees: 1952 (All-Star)

Games: 141 • **Batting Average: .293** • At-Bats: 553 • **Hits: 162 (10th in AL)** • Doubles: 31 (seventh in AL) • **Runs: 86 (10th in AL)**• Home Runs: 17 • **RBI: 74** • Total Bases: 256 (sixth in AL)

In 1949 Casey Stengel was named the manager of the Yankees, and one of his first moves was benching Bauer against right-handed pitching and using Gene Woodling as his platoon partner.

Woodling and Bauer probably became the most prolific platoon in baseball history with each of them having long and successful careers with the Yankees. While it was going on, each howled often to the press about not playing every day.

"Years later we both looked at it as the best thing for our careers," Bauer said.

Woodling, in fact, was still playing for the Mets under Stengel again at the age of 40 in 1962. Casey put his former platoon left-handed hitter in the lineup as a starter in both games of a double-header.

"That nearly killed me," Woodling later said.

Woodling retired from the game shortly thereafter.

Bauer's craggy face was a tipoff to the way he played the game: intense, hard, determined, all out, as if each July game was the seventh game of the World Series.

"If you weren't going to play the game hard, what the hell was the use of playing at all?" he once said.

Bauer, a three-time All-Star, was always one of those guys who seemed to play better when the game or the season was on the line. He was a solid hitter with a lifetime .277 average and 164 homers, a strong runner and an excellent fielder.

The 1951 World Series against the neighborhood New York Giants, who had defeated the Brooklyn Dodgers in that famous Shot Heard 'Round The World playoff game in which Bobby Thomson homered off Ralph Branca, was one of Bauer's best shows.

"I hit that three-run triple off Dave Koslo that gave us the sixth game and the Series win and then I made the last catch on my ass to end it," Bauer said.

The Yankees took a 4-1 lead into the ninth inning of the sixth game of that Series. The Giants rallied for two runs, and Giants manager Leo Durocher called backup catcher Sal Yvars, whom he hadn't spoken to in two months, out of the bullpen to pinch hit.

"Durocher was mad at me because I had talked back to him one time," Yvars recalled as he puffed on one of his ever-present cigars in his Valhalla, New York home. "I was just sitting out there getting the sun. Then I heard the phone ring, and they told me Leo wanted me to hit."

Yvars jogged into the Giants dugout, grabbed a bat and faced hard-throwing lefthander Bob Kuzava. He ripped a line drive to right.

"The ball was curving away from Bauer, and I thought it would make it to the wall. I could run pretty good and I figured I had a game-winning triple," Yvars said.

"I started toward the line," Bauer recalled. "I wasn't sure I could reach it. The ball seemed to be sailing away from me. I just leaned down at the last instant, stuck out my glove and got it. I must have slid another few feet on my ass with the ball sticking out of my glove."

Yvars has made a long career as an after dinner speaker telling tales about that one line drive that Bauer picked off the grass.

"The World Series was always so much fun for me," said Bauer. "You play all year to prove you are the best. That's what you want to show everybody."

Bauer played in nine World Series, batted .245 and collected a streak, getting a hit in 17 straight contests.

"That's something I'm real proud of," he said. "You want to show that consistency. That's what the game is all about."

He got some unwanted publicity in 1957 at Billy Martin's birthday party at the Copacabana in New York. Somebody knocked out a heckler. Many suggested Bauer was the culprit. He denies it. "The bouncer did it," he smiles.

He managed Kansas City and Baltimore after ending his playing career, earning great loyalty from his players and a fierce sense of competition from all his teams.

"I never wanted to be beaten because my guys didn't play hard," he said. "If the talent isn't there, it isn't there. But you didn't want to lose because your guys didn't put out."

Bauer remains close to his children and grandchildren, most of whom live in the Kansas City area. He loves to regale them with tales about his playing days, especially those World Series events and the seven championship rings he collected in nine tries at the title.

"When I was a kid growing up I didn't have much of an education. Then the war came along and I was in my middle 20s when I got out. I didn't know what the hell I would do if I didn't make it in baseball. In my day it was all about survival. If you didn't have an education you played sports or worked in a factory. I didn't want to work in a factory," he said.

Bauer has recognized the change in the game as a result of the huge salaries now being paid to big-league ballplayers.

"Most of them make a hell of a lot more in one year than I made it my entire career," he said. "I'm not jealous. They deserve what they can get. I fought hard to make what I got. I'll tell you one thing. They didn't have the kind of team and the kind of closeness we had on the Yankees. I've been friends with some of these guys I played with for 50 years now. I'm damn proud of that."

If any player identified the Yankees in those hard-nosed winning seasons of the late 1940s and 1950s it had to be Hank Bauer. He knew the difference between winning and losing. Nobody had better fool with his money.

BOB
CERV

It was always his 10 children that gave a story about Bob Cerv a little extra juice in his playing days. Now, at 77, there are also 30 grandchildren to talk about and his three great-grandchildren.

"I got all 10 of my kids through college," he said. "That's my finest accomplishment."

He is still near home in Lincoln, Nebraska, visiting with the grandchildren, driving golf balls huge distances, attending card shows with so many questions about teammates Mickey Mantle and Roger Maris and waiting for that occasional visit back to Yankee Stadium for an Old Timers event.

Cerv played 12 seasons in the big leagues with a .276 average in 829 games. His best seasons were actually with Kansas City with 38 homers in 1958 and 20 in 1959. Yet, he still considers himself a Yankee.

"Whenever I get up to New York for an Old Timers thing or a card show or anything and I'm walking down the street, some guy always yells, 'Hi, Bob. Hi Bob. We remember you with the Yankees.' That always gets me after all these years," he said.

Cerv had one of those faces and bodies that never could be forgotten. At six feet and 200 pounds, he always appeared to be

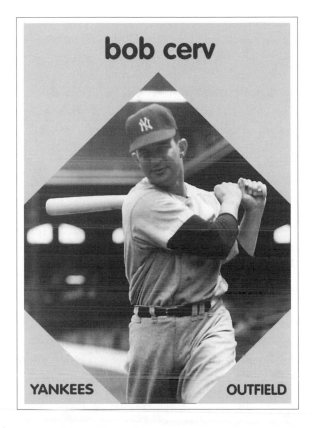

SEASONS WITH YANKEES: 1951-56; 1960; 1961-62

Best Season with Yankees: 1955

Games: **55** • Batting Average: **.341** • At-Bats: **85** • Hits: **29** • Runs: **17** • Home Runs: **3** • RBI: **22** •

squeezed into his uniform or his street clothes. His appearance was hard and a little fleshy with a neck that always seemed to be bursting from his shirt collar.

His first Yankee turn from 1951 through 1956 earned him four World Series rings and five pennants with more bench time as an outfield backup and pinch hitter than playing time. He had a vicious right-handed swing and often crushed line drives that made infielders wince when they collected them. He batted .341 in 55 games in 1955 and .304 in 54 games in 1956. He also collected eight World Series appearances, including the 1960 Series with the Yankees in which he collected five hits.

Cerv had been a baseball and basketball-star at the University of Nebraska and then played with Joe DiMaggio in his last year and Mickey Mantle in his first in 1951.

He was manager Casey Stengel's ace in the hole when opponents tried to shut off the Yankee right field home run power with left-handed pitching in the Stadium. Cerv presented a challenge for the opposition not only with his bat but with his fierce competitive attitude.

"That was just the Yankee way," he said.

He was sold to the A's in 1957, brought back to the Yankees in 1960 and claimed by the expansion Los Angeles Angels in 1961.

"The Yankees brought me back in May of 1961. That was the home run year of Maris and Mantle. I knew Mickey well from all my years with the Yankees and I knew Roger well. I had played with him in Kansas City. We were a lot alike, just small-town Midwestern guys who did our jobs and let others make the noise," Cerv said.

When the famous 1961 home run race heated up in late June, Maris and Mantle moved in with Cerv in a cozy apartment in Queens.

"I was like their father figure. I did all the shopping and cooking. I ran the place. I just told them both they could only stay there if they followed the rules—keep it clean, no women and no press. We spent a lot of nights just sitting together in the living room watching some television comedy and sipping a beer," Cerv said.

Cerv finished his career with the expansion Houston Colt 45s in 1962 and then retired.

"I was 36 years old, I had a lot of injuries, a broken jaw, a broken toe, a bad shoulder, pulled muscles that I played through. It was time to go," he said.

He became a college baseball coach at John F. Kennedy College in Wahoo, Nebraska, with more than a thousand of his college kids going into professional baseball. He also coached amateur teams in Liberal, Kansas, and a couple of significant major leaguers. Mike Hargrove, a long-time manager at Cleveland and Baltimore, and Ron Guidry, the great Yankee lefthander of the late 1970s, came out of Cerv's program.

Cerv said his greatest thrill in life, outside of his marvelous family, was just wearing that Yankee uniform.

"You just know when you put those pinstripes on you are carrying that tradition forward," Cerv said. "There's nothing like it, and it really stays with you for all your life. I played for Kansas City, Los Angeles and Houston, but nobody remembers that. I check into a hotel or make a restaurant reservation and it always is, 'Hey, you're the guy with the Yankees.' Then they start asking about Mickey and Roger."

Even all these years later, Cerv still has a soft spot in his heart for Maris.

"It was just a remarkable feat, that season, those home runs, all that Babe Ruth pressure, it was amazing he survived it all," Cerv said. "I think what Roger did that year under those conditions was something that has to be studied and appreciated more. I don't care how many home runs [Mark] McGwire or [Barry] Bonds hit, that will never equal what Roger did."

The baseball All-Stars get the big salary and the media attention. The spear carriers, the backup guys, the able substitutes when the stars can't make it, are the keys to winning seasons.

Baseball isn't football or basketball with a coasting season and an intense playoff. Baseball is a marathon from early February in spring training to the chill of an October World Series.

While the stars get the attention, the subs make the operation really work.

"I never regretted not playing every day with the Yankees. Maybe I would have made more money on another team ($30,000 was his top salary) but I certainly wouldn't have the success I had with these World Series rings and that Yankee identification. If I wasn't a Yankee I'd walk down the street and nobody would know my name," he said.

Bob Cerv is a contented man with his Yankee success, his World Series rings, his association with a couple of the game's greats in Maris and Mantle and the kids he steered into higher positions in the game.

"Just don't forget the joys of my family," he said. "Phyllis and I are celebrating our 56th wedding anniversary. That's a pretty good streak all by itself. We were married April 1, 1947. I don't think a lot of guys in baseball can say that," Cerv said.

He was a tough guy, a tough hitter, a sure-handed outfielder and a leader on those great Yankee teams of the 1950s and 1960s.

He is also a father, grandfather and great grandfather of note. For that alone, Bob Cerv is to be admired and respected.

BUD
DALEY

Leavitt Leo Daley was born October 7, 1932 in Orange, California. The doctors were a little off center with the instruments when they tried to bring him into the world. They damaged his right arm.

That should have ended any chance of a baseball career for a kid who was soon growing up as Bud Daley. He was too determined to let something like a deformed right arm stop him from achieving his dream of pitching in the major leagues.

"It always took a little convincing when I came to different teams," he said.

"They soon saw that I could get people out and I could field my position. I just had to hold the glove a little sideways on my right hand. I played 10 years in the big leagues with a lot of guys. I bet very few ever remember anything different about me."

Daley won 16 games twice for Kansas City before the Yankees brought him to New York in 1961, the famed Maris/Mantle home run season.

"I played with Roger on four clubs: Indianapolis, Cleveland, Kansas City and the Yankees," Daley said. "I didn't think he would hit a lot of home runs. Nobody did. He just had that beautiful line drive swing. I thought he would be a high average hitter. That all changed, I guess, when he came to New York."

SEASONS WITH YANKEES: 1961-64

Best Season with Yankees: 1961

Games: 23 • **Record 8-9** • ERA 3.96 • **Innings Pitched: 129 $^2/_3$** • Hits Allowed: 127 • **Strikeouts: 83** • Walks: 51

Yankee manager Casey Stengel saw the power in Roger's bat and pushed him to pull more for the short right field wall at the Stadium. He went from 16 homers to 39 in his first year as a Yankee and on to the record-breaking 61 in 1961.

"They started me as a left-handed relief pitcher at Cleveland. Cleveland had two of the best, Don Mossi and Ray Narleski, so there wasn't a lot of work for me," Daley recalled. "I realized I wouldn't be making much of a career that way."

Daley started 10 games for Cleveland before moving on to Kansas City where he won 16 games in 1959 and 16 again in 1960 for the lowly A's.

The Yankees had long looked on the A's as their big-league farm club and manager Casey Stengel took notice of Daley's skills in handling left-handed hitters, especially those who wanted to pull a ball into the nearby Stadium seats.

Stengel pushed for Daley but by the time the Yankees finally acquired the curveball-throwing lefthander in 1961, Stengel was on his way to managing the crosstown New York Mets.

Daley was 8-9 in 1961 with the Yankees in 23 games under new manager Ralph Houk and 7-5 in the second straight pennant-winning season of 1962. He pitched in two Series games in 1961 and one in 1962.

"That 1961 season with the Yankees was just an experience nobody can forget," he said. "With Mickey and Roger hitting home runs almost every day and the crowds of reporters around them all the time, the rest of us were pretty well forgotten. I didn't mind that. I was never a guy who craved publicity. I just liked to go out there and pitch. I enjoyed the competition more than anything else. When you pitched a good ball game and handled some good hitters, that was enough for me. One thing about pitching for the Yankees, everything seemed bigger than it was."

With all the turmoil around the Yankees as a result of the 1961 home run season, Daley was hardly appreciated for what he contributed. He pitched in turn, he usually went deep into the game saving Houk's bullpen, and he rarely complained when a start was skipped.

That was the season Whitey Ford really became a Hall of Fame pitcher, when Houk moved him from a five-game rotation into a four-game rotation. Ford started 39 games, pitched 283 innings, won 25 games while losing only four and led the Yankees to the pennant.

While Maris with his 61 homers and Mantle with his 54 got all the media, it was the pitching and defense that made the 1961 New York Yankees one of the greatest teams of all time.

"Our defense and pitching is what won it for us," Houk said years ago while reviewing that season. "You can have all the hitting in the world and you still won't win. Baseball is a low-scoring game. The runs you save with good pitching and good defense are just as important as the runs you score."

Daley was a control pitcher with good breaking stuff. He got a lot of ground balls, and his defense was important to his success. The Yankee infield of Moose Skowron, Bobby Richardson, Tony Kubek and Cletis Boyer was as good a defensive four as the game has seen.

"I always felt enormous confidence out there with those guys behind me," Daley said.

Daley had problems with his elbow in 1963 after starting on a freezing night and was out most of the year with bone chips. He started back up in 1964 as a spot starter and reliever.

"My arm just continued to get weaker and weaker and there was more pain in my elbow," he said. "I knew I just couldn't do it any more. You can't kid yourself in baseball. The hitters tell you when it is time to go."

He was only 31 years old when his career ended with 60 wins and 64 losses. He also won the final game of the 1961 World Series against Cincinnati after Ralph Terry was lifted by Houk. Daley shut down the Reds without a run in six and two-thirds innings.

"I just enjoyed pitching so much," he said. "I never made any money [$22,000 was his tops] but I had so much fun and met so many great guys. It's a nice memory to think that I played with Mickey and Roger and Whitey and all the rest of those great Yankees."

Daley has four children, seven grandchildren and a great grand-child now. He remembers what it was like when his career ended.

"I couldn't stay home thinking about it," he said. "I had too many mouths I had to feed, including my own. I got a job in sales in Los Angeles. That kept us going for a lot of years."

One of his children had moved out to Wyoming, and Daley and his wife, Dorothy, moved out there some 20 years ago.

"There's only one sport in Wyoming, that's football. Nobody knew or cared that I played baseball—even with the Yankees. That was fine. We just enjoyed the outdoors, the hunting and the fishing," he said.

Daley got a job working at a golf club, and he still plays as much as he can. He also travels occasionally to visit children and grandchildren and gets back to New York for a card show or baseball event.

"I have about a four or five handicap in golf and I can still hit a ball pretty far lefthanded," he said.

"The bone chips and the elbow don't bother me much now, and I have a lot of friends that I play with regularly."

It was remarkable more than four decades ago to see Bud Daley take the mound and fire off a pitch against the best hitters in the game without being able to straighten out his right arm.

In the best of times for the hardiest of souls, the game is pretty tough.

"I had pitched for so many years and I had been successful all the way up so it never was much of a big deal for me," he said. "It still isn't."

Bud Daley had 60 big-league wins. Most guys with a deformed arm like his never would have shown up in a big-league uniform. That World Series victory also puts him in a special category.

"I look at the guys today and the money they make and I think maybe I came along a little too early," he said. "…I have a lot of great memories."

Leavitt Leo Daley is a World Series winner. A lot of guys who can straighten out both arms never can say that.

SPARKY LYLE

He was always the life of the party, even if there was no party. Sparky Lyle was the kind of guy all the other players on the Yankees dreamed of being. He was loved and lovable. He laughed loudest when the jokes were on him. He quickly recognized that baseball was a game, dammit, a game, and that lives were never lost when a hitter slapped a double off him.

He could also pitch like hell with a slider that could bite the pants off most opposing batters.

Lyle would sit naked on a birthday cake or show up in a full body cast at spring training or tweak the owner or the manager with a funny line or quickie nickname.

Then he would be called on in the eighth or ninth inning of a crucial game, stroll into the infield with a jacket over his arm, approach the mound like a farmer approaching a field in harvest and settle matters in a hurry.

"The idea was to find out who won or lost so I always pitched fast," Lyle said.

He is now the manager of the Somerset Patriots in Central New Jersey, an independent club in the Atlantic League, with a new five-year contract taking him through 2007.

NEW YORK YANKEES

SPARKY LYLE

PITCHER

SEASONS WITH YANKEES: 1972-78

Best Season with Yankees: 1977 (Cy Young Award winner; sixth in MVP voting; All-Star)

Games: 72 (first in AL) • **Record: 13-5** • Saves: 26 (second in AL) • **ERA: 2.17** • Innings Pitched: 137 • **Hits Allowed: 131** • Strikeouts: 68 • **Walks: 33**

"These kids are professional players but they haven't been drafted by big-league clubs," he said. "They come here with the idea that they can impress somebody and get picked up by a big-league club so they can start making their millions."

Lyle said a lot of the kids on his team don't know much about his own brilliant pitching career.

"Ahh, they just come here, a little stuck on themselves, and somebody tells them something about me or they read something in a little newspaper when they want to read about themselves," he said. "Then one of them will walk up to me once in a while and say, 'Hey, skip, you were pretty good.' I just laugh."

Albert Walter Lyle—born July 22, 1944 in DuBois, Pennsylvania, a blue-collar town in the western part of the state—was as good as it gets in relief pitching with 238 saves in 16 years.

Lyle's father was a carpenter, and they often played together on local teams before young Albert—Sparky because his mother thought he was a sparkling child—started showing serious potential.

Lyle made it to the 1967 Impossible Dream team of the Red Sox, led by Hall of Famer Carl Yastrzemski, and pitched successfully in Boston through 1971. The Red Sox thought they were a hitter away from a title when they sent Lyle to the Yankees for Danny Cater.

Not much changed in Boston, but the Yankees started moving out of the gloom they had been in for 10 years. Ralph Houk made Lyle his closer, and he picked up a league-leading 35 saves in 1972.

After that it was all uphill for Lyle and the Yankees in the next half dozen years as the team moved back to its manifest destiny as the tops in the game and Lyle was recognized as the game's best relief pitcher.

Lyle was not only a key guy on the 1975 challengers, the pennant winners of 1976 and the World Champions of 1977, he was the best entertainment in town. Lyle, outfielder Lou Piniella, third baseman Graig Nettles and pitcher Catfish Hunter led a running, ripping dialogue on team buses, in hotel lobbies, around clubhouses and on the field that kept teammates loose and in stitches. For sportswriters it helped fill notebooks.

Lyle won 13 games and saved 26 in his Cy Young year of 1977 as the Yankees won their first World Series in 15 years.

They showed Lyle their appreciation for that incredible season by signing Rich (Goose) Gossage as their stopper and confining Lyle to a set-up role. It just broke his heart.

"Well, if you had me in the bullpen throwing that 78-mile-per-hour-slider and Goose in the bullpen throwing that 98-mile-per-hour heat, who would you pick?" he laughed.

It just didn't figure. Goose helped the Yankees win in 1978, and Lyle moved on to Texas, Philadelphia and the White Sox for his final years. He finished after the 1982 season with a 99-76 mark.

"I got a job like Mickey Mantle's at the Claridge Casino in Atlantic City playing golf with the rich guys, had some fun with those Miller Lite commercials, did a lot of card shows and fantasy camps and went on with the retirement stuff."

Lyle felt an awful lot of pain as the Yankees sort of ignored him through the years.

"It was as if I had fallen off the face of the earth," he said. "I was never invited down to spring training, I was never offered a job by the organization, I was never part of George's [Steinbrenner] club."

Lyle had worked his top salary up to $300,000 a year so he really didn't need a $50,000-a-year baseball job for survival. He simply wanted a little appreciation for his efforts on the field and the tickets he sold for the team as the comedy leader of a great club.

"I knew I was done when it happened. I still thought maybe I could teach a kid the slider. Maybe I talked too much and stood up to them more than they would have liked," he said.

Lyle and his wife, Mary, have three sons and live comfortably in Central New Jersey in the town of Voorhees. At 59 he is not much heavier than he was as a pitcher, six foot one and 185 pounds. His flowing mustache is gray now, and his thinning hair is all white.

"I really like this managing thing," he said. "I didn't think I would, but the kids try hard and play with a lot of enthusiasm. I still pitch a little BP [batting practice] and once in a while I can unload a good slider that causes a little surprise."

He admits that having fun around the game was almost as important to him as winning the World Series. He is just a guy who seems to slide through life without a care, laughing as often as he can, and making others laugh.

The sessions on the Yankee team bus in those glorious days in the late 1970s should have been taped and collected. They are funnier than anything Jay Leno or David Letterman could ever manage.

"I've been back to a couple of Old Timer days or we gather together at some card shows with a lot of the guys," he said. "It doesn't take long. Somebody makes a crack, and we are off and running."

Lyle hasn't sat naked on any birthday cakes for his Patriots team yet. After all, he is the skipper and pushing 60 years old. Then again, they haven't won yet, either. A seven-layer chocolate cake would be just about right.

ART
DITMAR

H e was the centerpiece in the most controversial managerial decision Casey Stengel made in his 30 years as a skipper. It reverberates even today when Art Ditmar shows up at a golf tournament or goes to a baseball card show or is stopped for an autograph.

"I was playing in one of those celebrity golf tournaments, and one of the sponsors came up to me and said how glad they were to have me playing, especially since I was the guy who gave up that winning World Series home run to Bill Mazeroski," Ditmar laughed.

Ralph Terry was the actual culprit in the 1960 World Series when Mazeroski, the flashy-fielding second baseman for the Bucs, hit a ninth-inning homer over Yogi Berra's head in left field for the victory. Radio announcer Chuck Thompson goofed on the call and said that it was Ditmar who surrendered the homer.

The Yankees scored 56 runs to Pittsburgh's 27 in the Series, but Pittsburgh won the seventh game 10-9 for the title. Ditmar had nothing to do with that one. Or maybe he did.

Ditmar, a husky righthander from Winthrop, Massachusetts, was 31 years old that season. He had a strong 15-9 mark with a 3.09 ERA to lead the Yankee staff as the Yankees won another runaway pennant.

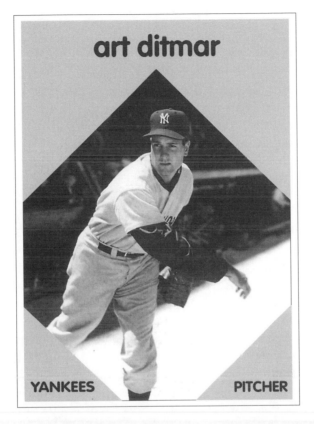

art ditmar

YANKEES   PITCHER

SEASONS WITH YANKEES: 1957-61

Best Season with Yankees: 1960

Games: 34 • **Record: 15-9 (fourth in Wins in AL)** • ERA: 3.06 (fourth in AL) • **Innings Pitched: 200** • Hits Allowed: 195 • **Strikeouts: 65** • Walks: 56

Whitey Ford was 12-9 in 33 games with a 3.08 ERA. He was 33 years old that season.

"There was a lot of fussing in the press about who would open the Series. Casey finally came up to me the day before and said, 'You deserve the start.' I was very pleased," he said.

Stengel knew the Pirates were a tough team with a lot of right-handed power in future Hall of Famer Roberto Clemente, Dick Stuart, the famed Dr. Strangeglove for his errant mitt, Dick Groat, Gino Cimoli and Maseroski. He wanted a righthander against them as he saved Ford for the Game 3 start in Yankee Stadium.

"I think Whitey also had a little bit of a tender arm and Casey was concerned that he couldn't start him three times if the Series went that far," said Ditmar.

Ditmar only lasted one-third of an inning in the opener. He surrendered three runs and the Yankees lost 6-4. Elroy Face, the great Pittsburgh screwball pitcher, saved the game.

In Game 2, Bob Turley pitched a strong game, and the Yankees exploded for 16 runs. Then Ford pitched the first of his two Series shutouts with a 10-0 win. With a 2-1 lead in the series and 30 runs scored in three games, the Yankees seemed ready to lock it up easily.

The forgotten fourth game was probably the difference as Vernon Law and reliever Face again outpitched the Yankees and Terry for a 3-2 Series tying win.

Ditmar could only get by an inning and a third in the fifth game as the Pirates won 5-2. His Series ERA of 21.60 was nothing to write home about.

"Maybe I would have done better if I had pitched in those games when we scored a bundle of runs," he said.

Ford pitched his second shutout in the sixth game to tie the Series, and Mazeroski ended it the next day with the home run, which nudged him into the Baseball Hall of Fame in Cooperstown 41 years later.

Ditmar became a marked man in Yankee lore after that Series. New manager Ralph Houk sent him on to Kansas City in the middle of the next season.

Ditmar ended his career after the 1962 season at Kansas City with a 72-77 mark in nine big-league seasons.

"I was a sinker ball pitcher and I was having a little trouble with my arm. [A's owner] Charlie Finley figured he could save some money so he let me go," Ditmar said.

His top salary was $30,000 in the big leagues, but Ditmar didn't see that as a financial problem.

"After all," he said, "I bought a nice house in Massachusetts for $12,000."

He soon became the baseball coach at American International College near his home in Springfield, Massachusetts and later moved on to Brook Park, Ohio, as the town's recreation director.

He and his wife, Diane, are the parents of four children. They have seven grandchildren. Ditmar and his wife now make their home next to a golf course in Myrtle Beach, South Carolina.

At the age of 74, he is a little heavier than in his pitching days of six foot two and 185 pounds but can still drive a golf ball a long way and stays close to his 14 handicap.

"We're doing OK. I got a couple of pensions from school, baseball and the city, and there's always social security. What probably has changed most because of the big salaries today is that everybody thinks we're millionaires," he said.

Living in South Carolina, he sees more Atlanta Braves games than any other team but still considers himself a Yankee booster.

"I still get a big kick getting back to New York and suiting up once in a while at Yankee Stadium for those Old Timer games," he said.

Ditmar never thinks about that 1960 Series unless he is asked. He also pitched in the 1957 and 1958 Series for the Yankees and didn't give up a run.

"Things like that happen in baseball," he said of the disappointing performance in 1960. "You just have to go out there the next time and start all over again. That's what I always tried to do."

When he looks back on that Series start more than 43 years ago after being asked, he sees no reason to second guess Stengel, as most of the baseball press did, on his decision to go with Ditmar over Ford as the first game Series starter.

"After all, I won more games than anybody that year, and the Pirates looked like a club I could handle," he said. "I'd go along with Casey's call any time. He was pretty damn successful."

Ditmar can hit a golf ball hard and far. Maybe things would have been different if the Yankees had hit a few balls hard and far for him in 1960.

ROLLIE SHELDON

His birth date is December 17, 1936. You could look it up. That's his real birth date. No kidding. He says that is what it reads on his birth certificate filed at city hall in Putnam, Connecticut.

All this fuss over a baseball player's birthday came about in 1961 when the best young pitcher in the Yankee spring training camp at St. Petersburg, Florida was Roland Frank Sheldon. He was good enough to win the James P. Dawson award, presented annually to the most outstanding rookie in the Yankee camp.

The tall righthander, who stood six foot four and weighed a spindly 185 pounds, impressed rookie manager Ralph Houk enough to win a spot in the Yankees' starting rotation along with future Hall of Famer Whitey Ford, Bill Stafford and Ralph Terry.

Sheldon, listed as 21 on the Yankee roster that spring when he really was 24, got off to a fine start. That was his undoing.

"A lot of the Connecticut sportswriters had covered me in high school," Sheldon said. "They knew how old I was. They started writing about it and telling the other sports writers."

He had served in the Air Force after high school, and when he got out and signed with the Yankees, he was told by a scout to fudge a little on the form the Yankees had him fill out.

SEASONS WITH YANKEES: 1961-65

Best Season with Yankees: 1961

Games: 35 • **Record: 11-5** • ERA: 3.60 • **Innings Pitched: 162 $^2/_3$** • Hits Allowed: 149 • **Strikeouts: 84** • Walks: 55

"I figured if they wouldn't give me a chance because I was 24 I'd better go along with the little fib," he said.

Baseball players have lied about their ages in perpetuity. One of the best baseball fake-age stories concerned Billy Bruton, a Detroit Tigers outfielder who retired at the alleged age of 41 after a dozen big-league seasons in 1964.

"I'm really 44," he announced at the retirement press conference, "and I want that baseball pension right away."

The real age was soon a reality on all the Yankee press releases about Sheldon as the fuss died down.

"When I first joined the Yankees I was just scared to death. You can't walk into the locker room at Yankee Stadium without your knees shaking. Even though I was older than anyone thought and I had been around to college and the Air Force, I was still nervous," he said.

The Yankee players, by tradition, didn't make it any easier. They simply abused every rookie who showed up in that inner sanctum.

"They just treat you like a batboy or something," he said. "I remember Whitey Ford asking me to get him a coke or Mickey Mantle asking for a towel. All the veteran players just take advantage of you and want to make fun of you."

Sheldon said he really got red-faced when he came to his locker after one game and a message was on his stool. It listed a phone number and said, "Call Mr. Bear right away."

"I went over to the clubhouse phone not knowing what this could possibly be, dialed the number and heard a guy on the other end say, 'Bronx Zoo.' Then I turned around and saw about a dozen players laughing at me," he said.

The major force behind these practical jokes was not Ford or Mantle or any other Yankee. It was usually Pete Sheehy, the clubhouse attendant who had been pulling these rituals around the Yankees ever since he joined the team in 1926.

Sheehy always thought if those jokes were good enough for the Babe Ruth/Lou Gehrig Yankees, they were certainly good enough for the Mickey Mantle/Whitey Ford Yankees.

"I got on to all this after a while," he said. "It stopped when I proved I belonged up there by winning a few ball games."

Sheldon had 21 starts in his rookie season, turned in an 11-5 mark with a 3.60 ERA, pitched well in his few relief assignments and seemed set for a long, prosperous Yankee career.

He slipped to 7-8 the following year with 16 starts and was 5-2 in 1964 after sitting out the 1963 season with injuries. Sheldon warmed up but did not get into the World Series in 1961 against Cincinnati or 1962 against the Giants. He was not eligible for the 1963 quickie against the Los Angeles Dodgers when Sandy Koufax, Don Drysdale, Johnny Podres and reliever Ron Perranoski made spaghetti out of Yankee bats in a four-game sweep. The Bronx Bombers scored all of four runs in four games against the Dodgers in that Series.

In 1964 Sheldon got into two Series games and didn't give the Cardinals a hit in two and two-thirds innings.

The following season, 1965, Sheldon's short Yankee career came to an end when he was traded to Kansas City along with Yankee backup catcher Johnny Blanchard.

"I pitched for Kansas City and Boston the following year and didn't do much. I got shuffled off to Buffalo by the Red Sox. Johnny Bench was in the league and he just tore it up. It was amazing to see a kid that good that young," said Sheldon.

He had settled in Lee's Summit, Missouri, by that time with his wife, Shirley Ann. They have four children and three grandchildren.

"I really like the area. We have a nice home, and the life is easy out here. Everybody knows I played for the Yankees, and that is what people want to talk about most," he said.

Sheldon got into the insurance business around the Kansas City area, did well and retired about 10 years ago.

"I watch baseball on television but I am really a lazy guy and don't travel around much or do anything too strenuous now. I play golf and I go fishing occasionally but I'm mostly around the house," he said.

Sheldon said it was fun to play with the Yankees and be a teammate of such great players as Mickey Mantle, Whitey Ford, Roger Maris and all the other Yankee stars of the time.

"I never made more than $18,000 a year playing baseball but that was probably an average salary at the time," he said. "I did play for three World Series teams and I think that is a pretty good record to have when you are in the big leagues only five years."

At the age of 67—that's right, 67 years old—Sheldon is comfortably content. A lazy retirement isn't all that bad.

RON BLOMBERG

I shoulda been a doctor and a lawyer like my parents wanted me to be," Ron Blomberg blurted out one day after a frustrating after-noon at bat with the Yankees.

Blomberg, a Jewish Yogi Berra with a sweet smile and an intense desire to please, was always saying funny things, sort of accidentally in a classic southern drawl.

Ronald Mark Blomberg of Atlanta, Georgia, joined the Yankees in 1969 as a 20-year-old with a L'il Abner body and the gee-whiz attitude to match.

Everything was an adventure for the kid from Georgia, especially the meal money on the road and the free lunches sportswriters were anxious to buy him just so they could hear his drawl.

His eating habits—two, three, four hamburgers at a sitting for a snack, huge portions of fries, donuts by the dozens and containers of Coke from the bottling plants in his native Georgia—were notable for the friendly kid.

"A lot of guys used to get on me about my eating but I never really gained weight. I seemed to have a huge appetite but I burned everything up," Blomberg said.

NEW YORK YANKEES

RON
BLOMBERG   DH

SEASONS WITH YANKEES: 1969-76

Best Season with Yankees: 1973

Games: 100 • Batting Average: .329 • At-Bats: 301 • Hits: 99 •
Runs: 45 • Home Runs: 12 • RBI: 57

Elston Howard, a Yankee coach and former catcher, took the kid under his wing. He tried to steer Blomberg away from the snacks table after a game.

"You keep this up and you'll weigh 400 pounds," Howard once chided Blomberg.

"Just then a guy walked into the clubhouse," Blomberg recalled. "He was huge, really huge."

Blomberg asked Howard who the fellow was. Howard looked over and saw Joe Black, once a great Brooklyn Dodger who had let himself gain an incredible amount of weight. He weighed nearly 400 pounds.

"That's you," said Howard, "in about 10 years."

At six foot one and 195 pounds, with huge shoulders, heavy thighs and strong forearms, Blomberg could drive a baseball as far and hard as anybody in the game in his time.

He had a .293 lifetime average in eight seasons with 52 home runs and only 134 strikeouts. He was a left-handed hitter who was labeled a platoon player early in his career, sort of the Gene Woodling to Hank Bauer's right-handed-hitting platoon partner.

"I don't know how that happened," he said. "I think I could have hit lefthanders if they had given me the chance. I never bailed out against lefties and I always hit them in school and in the minors."

Yankee manager Ralph Houk kept Blomberg away from lefthanders as often as he could. Not much changed after Bill Virdon became the new Yankee manager in 1974.

Blomberg's playing time decreased under Virdon and ended completely in 1976 under Billy Martin's first tour of Yankee duty.

Blomberg, a designated hitter and first baseman, was placed in left field for a spring training game in March of 1977 just to get some at-bats. He had missed all of the 1976 season, except for two at-bats in one game, with shoulder injuries. Now Martin was anxious to see if he had anything left.

Blomberg awkwardly chased a fly ball at the Red Sox's Winter Haven park, tore up his knee in the crash and never could drive a ball much after that.

"I don't know why I had a lot of injuries, but I did," he said. "Whenever I got an injury it seemed that it would be a serious one, and I was out a long time."

He got a $300,000 free agent contract with the White Sox in 1978 but hit only .231 in 61 games before he hung it up.

"Then I had to go home and give up the fantasy life of a baseball player and get into a regular life," he said. "That's never easy."

Blomberg was such a cooperative, pleasant and friendly kid in his Yankee days that the press accepted his foibles and played up his power. Every so often he would unload a big home run. Stories would appear that he was on his way to greatness, he would be the popular Jewish first baseman in New York, the guy who stayed with the Yankees the way Hank Greenberg, the Jewish first baseman from the Bronx, chose not to do. Greenberg's reason when he turned down a Yankee offer and chose to go to Detroit was simple. It could be spelled out in two words: Lou Gehrig.

Blomberg had no such challenge. The Yankees were at their lowest when he joined them. The team, the press and certainly the large Jewish New York population wanted this kid to make it big. He could only make it small.

"I look back now and I wonder why I didn't do what I could to become better. The injuries had a lot to do with it. The platooning hurt. Maybe it just wasn't meant to be," he said.

Blomberg gained one moment of lasting fame on Opening Day at Fenway Park in Boston in 1973 with the New England wind blowing across his face. He got up as a designated hitter against Luis Tiant and walked on a 3-2 pitch with the bases loaded. It was baseball's first designated hitter at-bat in what is now a 30-year experiment.

"I got my name in a lot of books for that and I am asked to a lot of card shows and I was even a question and answer on *Jeopardy* because I was the first," he said.

There are always people stopping him on the streets or in hotel lobbies or at airports saying, "You were the first."

Blomberg and his second wife, Beth, live outside Atlanta in Roswell, Georgia. He began a career consulting company with help from his wife's parents about 20 years ago that proved quite successful.

"We helped people get jobs," he said. "I knew a lot about that."

He also worked for a hair replacement company after his thick dark hair began going south. He is now completely bald but looks as stylish as his many contemporaries who adopt that style to disguise loss of hair.

"I still get back to New York on business occasionally or for a Yankee event. People are always yelling at me. They remember. I just loved playing with the Yankees and appreciated the other guys on the team. I was really close to a lot of them—Ellie Howard, Thurman Munson, Bobby Bonds, Roy White. I really enjoy seeing them to this day. I am also close to Phil Niekro down here in Atlanta. We do a lot of things together."

When you talk to Ron Blomberg it is like talking to Marlon Brando in his movie role when Brando bellows, "I coulda been somebody. I coulda been a contendah."

Ron Blomberg coulda been Hank Greenberg. He coulda been a champion. Injuries, illness and left-handed pitchers probably did him in.

He also coulda been a doctor. At least his son, Adam, who is in medical school at Miami, will be one. There are no lawyers in his family so far, but his daughter is only 17.

DON
BAYLOR

Don Baylor was sitting on the Mets bench prior to a late spring training game in March of 2003 at the team's headquarters in Port St. Lucie, Florida.

He looked across the field at another special spring Mets coach, Hall of Fame pitcher Tom Seaver.

"Tom and I were the two guys on the top step of the Boston dugout that day in 1986. We thought we'd be the first on the field to congratulate our Red Sox teammates for winning the World Series," he laughed.

Instead, Mookie Wilson's ground ball climbed through Bill Buckner's glove, the Mets won the game and closed out the Series the next day with a seventh game win. Boston still hasn't won a Series since Babe Ruth pitched them—yes, pitched them—to their last one in 1918 with two victories.

Baylor spent 19 years in the big leagues but seems to receive the most attention for his three seasons with the Yankees from 1983 to 1985.

It was Baylor who served as the enforcer on the team, the guy the other players turned to in distress, the class act among a group of crybabies annoyed at the owner's mishandling of the club. George

YANKEES

DON BAYLOR

SEASONS WITH YANKEES: 1983-85

Best Season with Yankees: 1983

Games: 144 • **Batting Average: .303** • At-Bats: 534 • **Hits: 162** • Runs: 82 • **Doubles: 33** • Home Runs: 21 • **RBI: 85** • Stolen Bases: 17 • **Hit By Pitch: 13 (2nd in AL)**

Steinbrenner was at his most loquacious and rambunctious during Baylor's years.

It came to a head in 1985 when Steinbrenner panicked at a 4-12 start, fired Yogi Berra, brought back unstable Billy Martin and saw the franchise travel on quicksand.

When the team was informed of the change, Baylor let his feelings be known by knocking over a food table and kicking a garbage can across the clubhouse floor.

"Ahh," Baylor laughed, "it didn't go very far."

Baylor hit .303, .262 and .231 in his three seasons with the Yankees. There was no sense that he was leading the team to a pennant but he was always leading the team in effort. It was just his way.

Baylor's contributions weren't always measured in baseball numbers. They came from his influence on others as a role model, leader and dedicated team player.

Just before the Mets left spring training for the 2003 season he revealed another part of his personality under great stress.

Baylor announced to his teammates and later to the press that he was suffering from multiple myeloma (bone marrow cancer) and would be undergoing chemotherapy to fight the disease early in the season. He didn't expect to miss any games as a Mets coach.

"Normally when you stand in against Nolan Ryan that probably should be your toughest challenge," he said. "In this game you always have different challenges. [It's absolutely a goal] to be here every day."

Don Edward Baylor was born June 28, 1949 in segregated Austin, Texas. He was the first African American to attend the all-white public schools of Austin and the first of his race to play on the high school baseball team at Austin High.

He was 17 when he signed with the Baltimore organization, won the batting title with a .346 mark and hit .369 and .333 with Stockton and Elmira before joining the Orioles in 1970. He stayed with the team through 1975, then moved to Oakland, California, the Yankees for those three years, Boston, Minnesota and finally Oakland again.

He recorded a .260 lifetime average over 19 seasons, hit 338 home runs, batted in 1,276 runs and stole 285 bases.

Perhaps his most significant statistic was his big-league-record 276 hit by pitches he recorded with his tough no-nonsense batting style.

"The pitcher always wants to push a batter off the plate," said Baylor. "I just wouldn't let them do that to me."

He had only one .300 year—with the Yankees in 1983—but was a force on seven postseason teams he played for, including three World Series teams.

When the new Colorado Rockies franchise began play in 1993 they selected Baylor as their first manager. He established the team, built its character and got close to winning in 1995 with a second-place finish.

He stayed in Colorado until 1998, moved over to Atlanta as a coach and became manager of the Cubs in 2000.

The goal there was simply to give the Cubs a World Series champion, something they hadn't accomplished since 1908 when the famed (Joe) Tinker, (Johnny) Evers and (Frank) Chance-led infield brought the north side of the Windy City a crown. For trivia buffs, of course, the third baseman on that team was Harry Steinfeldt.

Baylor finished third with the 2001 Cubs but was fired in the middle of the 2002 season when all signs pointed to the Cubs keeping their non-Series winning streak going.

"I understood that," he said, during a spring training break. "That's what the game is all about. If you don't win you get fired. Sometimes if you do win, you get fired."

He and his wife, Rebecca make their home in La Quinta, California and in his native Austin, Texas. They have one grown son, Don Jr.

Baylor said he was thrilled to be back in the game when Mets manager Art Howe, a former coach for Baylor in Colorado, hired him for the Mets job.

"When I was playing I always wanted to be the best I could and help my team win," he said. "When I was coaching or managing I just wanted to make the team better in any way I could. I wanted to contribute."

He certainly contributed much on and off the field in his three seasons with the Yankees as a leader and role model for younger, undisciplined players in learning how the game should be played.

"It was just natural for me to play hard," he said. "I think I learned that as a kid playing in the 100-degree heat in Texas. You just played hard. You never looked for excuses."

Now he is facing the most important challenge in his life with bone marrow cancer. This is a guy who has been up to every challenge. Always. He has the perfect attitude to conquer this one.

BILL WERBER

H e is the oldest living former Yankee at 95 years old, and maybe still one of the brightest.

Bill Werber traveled with the 1927 Yankees, maybe baseball's best team ever, as a college student on vacation from Duke University, and signed with them in time to join the team for the 1930 season.

He came back to the Yankees in 1933, was traded to the Boston Red Sox and played for the Philadelphia A's, Cincinnati Reds and New York Giants in a career that covered 11 seasons. He hit .271, stole 215 bases and starred on the 1940 World Champion Reds with a .370 mark.

After his 1942 season with the Giants and with World War II raging, Werber retired to enter the insurance business.

"The first year out of the game I made over $100,000. That was pretty good since I was only making $22,000 in baseball," he said.

Born June 20, 1908 in Berwyn, Maryland, Werber now lives in a retirement home in Charlotte, North Carolina near the home of his daughter, Pat Bryant, and close to the campus of Duke University. He starred as a baseball and basketball player at Duke more than 70 years ago. He was Duke's first All-America basketball star.

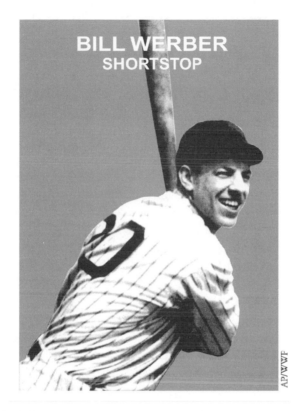

BILL WERBER
SHORTSTOP

AP/WWF

SEASONS WITH YANKEES: 1930; 1933

Best Season with Yankees: 1930

Games: 4 • **Batting Average: .286** • At-Bats: 14 • **Hits: 4** • Runs
5• **Home Runs: 0** • RBI: 2

"The Yankees wanted to sign me, so during the 1927 season when I was off from school I traveled with the team. I used to play bridge with Babe Ruth, Lou Gehrig and Bill Dickey. I always played with Ruth, and Dickey and Gehrig played together," he said.

They played mostly on the trains as the Yankees traveled around the league.

"As soon as we boarded the train Babe would order ice and glasses and pull out the bottle of Seagram's from his suitcase. He would drink it real slowly throughout the game. We only played for a few pennies. Babe would start needling Lou and drinking a little more, and that's how we knew the game was almost over," he said.

Werber said that Babe was always friendly with his teammates, with the press and with the fans. Gehrig wasn't friendly with anybody.

"I think Dickey was the only teammate he ever really talked to. Actually I think he really was a momma's boy. That one spring when I went to spring training with the Yankees he set his mother up in a room right next to his in the Don Cesar hotel. Every night they were together," he said.

Werber recalled that Ruth would make a grand entrance into the clubhouse, shouting at the players, throwing off his jacket, calling for a sandwich as soon as he got in.

"Where's the Dago?" Ruth would yell as he searched out one of his playful teammates, Tony Lazzeri, an Italian star from San Francisco.

"Babe had a lot of funny things going all the time with Tony, like hot foots or putting stuff in his underwear or nailing his shoes to the ground. Babe once cut off Tony's spikes, and he was really mad at that," Werber said.

A Jewish ball player born Hymie Solomon—now known as Jimmy Reese—joined the Yankees in 1930 and immediately became Babe Ruth's best pal.

"Where's the Jew, where's the Jew?" Ruth would yell when he entered the clubhouse after Reese joined the team.

Reese and Ruth roomed together on the road in 1930 and 1931. Reese later described his experiences as Ruth's roommate by saying, "I didn't room with Babe Ruth, I roomed with his suitcase."

The tales Reese collected about the Yankees and especially the Babe he would tell to players on the California Angels—especially his best pal, Hall of Famer Nolan Ryan, about half a century later.

"I just loved playing with the Babe on the Yankees," Werber said.

"He was an incredible character and an amazing player. He didn't remember names or faces, you know. One time we had a guy on the club named Myles Thomas. He had been with the Yankees a couple of years and one day in the lobby of the hotel in Boston, Lazzeri grabs the kid as he is walking around. He ushers him over to the Babe and introduces him as a new guy on the team just signed out of Harvard. 'Welcome, keed,' the Babe says. He had no idea the guy had been around two seasons."

In 1934 Werber was playing third for the Red Sox and the Babe hit a long triple.

"He slid [into] third, and I could smell a little alcohol on his breath. It wasn't all that bad. The worst guy for that was Paul Waner. He used to drink so much that you could smell him going around first toward third if he hit a triple. Somehow Waner kept hitting and got in the Hall of Fame," said Werber.

Werber recalled one of the saddest days he ever experienced in baseball. It was during that 1934 season when Ruth was playing left field for the Yankees in Boston's Fenway Park.

"I hit a bullet line drive out that way. You have to remember this was the end of Babe's career. He couldn't run much any more. The ball just sailed under his glove, and I made it to third on a hit that should have been a single. I was with the Red Sox, the home team, and he was with the visiting Yankees but the fans just started booing the Babe for not catching the ball. He had been such a great star in Boston and had done so much for the game in New York. How could people be so cruel?"

Werber said he still watches baseball and stays up with the Yankees and the Reds, his two favorite teams.

"Actually I met Mr. Steinbrenner a few years ago when he came down here to North Carolina for some charity golf event. We had breakfast together after somebody introduced me as a former Yankee. He was very friendly. He even picked up the check. We tried going down early for breakfast the next day, but it didn't work. He was already gone," said Werber.

Werber was with the Reds in 1940 when a young backup catcher to future Hall of Famer Ernie Lombardi named Willard Hershberger committed suicide by cutting himself repeatedly while he sat in the tub of his hotel room.

"That was very sad, but I can't say I was too surprised. He was a very intense, introverted guy, always worried about everything," Werber said. "You can't play baseball that way. You can't live that way."

Werber has lived a wonderfully contented and satisfying life for more than half a century after he left the game, with the love of family, friends and fans. He still gets occasional baseball cards of himself to sign and carefully inscribes all of them with his fine penmanship.

"I still can read and write and I enjoy being outside walking around when the weather is good," he said.

He is a major attraction in the senior residence he now lives in and can entertain the other residents with tales of the Babe, Lou Gehrig and the Yankees for hours. His daughter, Pat, says her dad stays up on the news but has a special place in his heart for the Yankees.

"He was very disappointed when the Yankees didn't make it to the World Series last year," she said in early 2003. "I think he is already planning on watching them in October of 2003."

Werber enjoyed every minute of his professional career, especially those Yankee days with Ruth, Gehrig, Dickey and all those other great Yankee stars.

"I won a World Series with Cincinnati but the Yankees spotted me first and gave me my chance in the big leagues. It was such a great thrill to work out with that 1927 club and finally make it to the Yankees in 1930. Yankee Stadium is like a landmark in this country," he said.

At the age of 95, Bill Werber is sort of a landmark himself.

RON
GUIDRY

He was at the Yankees spring training camp on one of the back diamonds at Legends Field in Tampa on a balmy Florida afternoon late in March of 2003.

When he finished showing a bunch of Yankee youngsters how to grip that slider and make it dance in the dirt before unsuspecting hitters, Ron Guidry stood in the shade and reminisced about those seasons some 25 years ago when he dominated the game.

"I can still throw the ball pretty good for a few hitters," he said, "but then the lack of stamina takes its toll."

Ronald Ames Guidry, nicknamed Gator by his teammates (for his back country Louisiana background) and Louisiana Lightning by the media (for his crackling fast ball and biting slider), still wasn't much over his pitching weight of 161 pounds on that five-foot-11 frame.

"George [Steinbrenner] is kind enough to invite me down here every spring so I get some work in for a few weeks and then spend the rest of the year hunting and fishing. We have a nice home so it is a pretty good life," he said.

Guidry made the Yankees after much controversy because he never looked the part of a power pitcher and left with even more

NEW YORK YANKEES

RON GUIDRY — PITCHER

SEASONS WITH YANKEES: 1975-88

Best Season with Yankees: 1978 (Cy Young Award winner; second in MVP voting; All-Star)

Games: 35 (ninth in AL) • **Record: 25-3 (first in W-L percentage; first in Wins)** • ERA: 1.74 (first in AL) • **Innings Pitched 273 $^2/_3$ (seventh in AL)** • Hits Allowed: 187 • **Strikeouts: 248 (second in AL)** • Walks: 72 • **Complete Games: 16 (seventh in AL)** • Shutouts: 9 (first in AL)

controversy because the Yankees figured he was finished, and Guidry didn't quite agree.

He was born August 28, 1950, in Lafayette, Louisiana. He spoke a patois of English and Cajun as a youngster around the family and neighbors with the French background.

Some teammates had trouble understanding the off-beat twang, but they quickly recognized that pitching style as soon as his thin body and rangy arms unloaded his fastball.

The Yankees were still in Shea Stadium while Yankee Stadium was being remodeled when Guidry joined the team late in 1975. There was a difference of opinion between GM Gabe Paul and manager Bill Virdon about whether this skinny kid could be a regular starter.

He started only one game in 1975 and none in 1976 with seven appearances before manager Billy Martin stuck his neck out for Guidry early in 1977.

He was 26 years old that summer, and Paul believed he needed more pitching in relief before he could become a starter.

"He has to build up his arm strength against big-league hitters," Paul insisted.

"He's ready now, and I'm going to use him in turn," insisted Martin.

He got 31 starts in 1977, won 16 games, beat the Dodgers in the World Series and established himself quickly as one of the best lefthanders in the game.

Ron Guidry may have had the best single season by any pitcher in the memorable 1978 season when the Yankees came from 14 games behind the Red Sox to win the pennant.

During that memorable season, he was 25-3 with a breathtaking 1.74 ERA, 248 strikeouts and nine shutouts. He was also the winner in the final playoff game against Boston 5-4 with reliever Goose Gossage getting the save by popping up future Hall of Famer Carl Yastrzemski for the final out.

"I guess that has to be looked at as my best game," Guidry said. "I may not have had my finest stuff, but it meant an awful lot. I guess a lot of guys still remember it."

That was the game won by Bucky Dent's three-run homer off Mike Torrez even though Reggie Jackson's home run really turned out to be the difference in the one-run game.

"I was pretty tired by then," Guidry said. "I had done a lot of pitching that year [273 innings] and I was a little weary going into that game."

Guidry rarely failed the Yankees in a big game throughout his 14 years with the club. He added two more 20-game winning seasons in 1983 and 1985. He turned in a majestic .651 winning percentage—just behind Whitey Ford's .690—with 170 wins and 91 losses.

His last two years were downers with a 5-8 mark in 1987 and 2-3 in only a dozen games in 1988.

He came to spring training in 1989 after some arm trouble. The Yankees couldn't see paying him the $300,000 he was making by then so they offered him a minor league job to see if he could still pitch.

"I wasn't going to the minors at that stage of my career," he said.

"I thought my arm was coming back and I was throwing well. I thought I deserved an opportunity to find out against big-league hitters."

The Yankees thought otherwise. In one of those classic baseball "What have you done for me lately?" stories, Guidry was sent packing.

It was a bitter experience for the guy who had anchored the pitching staff for 10 seasons and collected Series victories in 1977, 1978 and 1981 against the Dodgers.

"I had been around long enough by then," Guidry said. "I knew how things worked. I was disappointed but I can't say I was very surprised."

He and his wife, Bonnie, parents of three children, enjoyed his new time at home and working the small farm they owned, did some traveling, and appreciated all the good years they had in New York.

After a few years away from the game and the cooling of tempers on all sides, Guidry was invited back to spring training with the Yankees to give some help to hopeful slider pitchers.

"I really enjoy working with the kids," he said. "A lot of people helped me along the way and I thought I could help other kids, especially with that pitch I lived off."

Guidry said he had no ambitions about coming back to baseball full time.

"This is just about enough for me, coming down here each year, working with the kids, fooling with some of my old teammates who may be around spring training and throwing a little BP until I get exhausted," he said.

With the new Hall of Fame veterans' committee setup, Guidry has gained much support for entry into the game's shrine. He doesn't expect it to happen but he welcomes the attention.

"When you are appreciated by your colleagues and your contemporaries that is enough of an honor," he said. "If the Hall of Famers think I'm worthy that will be a great thrill. If not, I'm sure my teammates will always remember what we did together."

Guidry was not one of those talkative rambunctious Yankees during the late 1970s on a team immortalized as The Bronx Zoo for the fighting between owner Steinbrenner, manager Martin, players Reggie Jackson, Lou Piniella, Thurman Munson and so many others.

"Some kids want to grow up to be ballplayers and some want to join the circus," said witty third baseman Graig Nettles. "I grew up to do both."

While others plotted as they sat in the back of Yankee charter flights or in the corner of the clubhouse, Guidry played chess quietly with sportswriters.

Then the Gator would take the mound the next day. Now you could hear the noise. It was usually 50,000 people screaming his name as he struck out another tough hitter in another key spot.

MIKE
TORREZ

He spent only 211 days with the Yankees—from April 27, 1977 when he was traded to them from Oakland in a deal for Dock Ellis to November 23 that same year. Then he signed with Boston as a free agent.

Still, for what he accomplished that season on and off the field and what the Yankees achieved against him the following October, Mike Torrez remains one of their more historic figures. His name will not be forgotten in Yankee lore.

"How many people know I caught the last out of the 1977 Series?" laughed Torrez, as he reminisced about his Yankee time and his Boston time the following year.

What Yankee fans remember—what Torrez can never forget—is that wimpy fly ball Bucky Dent hit over the wall at Fenway Park on October 2, 1978. It gave the Yankees a 3-2 lead in the playoff game for the AL East title. The Yankees won the game 5-4.

Torrez had a 2-0 lead with two out in the top of the seventh. Chris Chambliss and Roy White got hits for the Yankees. Manager Don Zimmer was so confident of Torrez's guts and skills, he had no one throwing in the bullpen.

NEW YORK YANKEES

MIKE TORREZ — PITCHER

AP/WWP

SEASONS WITH YANKEES: 1977

Best Season with Yankees: 1977

Games: 31 • Record: 14-12 • ERA: 3.82 • Innings Pitched: 217 • Hits Allowed: 212 • Strikeouts: 90 • Walks: 75 • Complete Games: 15

Bucky Dent was the next batter. He fouled the first ball off his foot. Next hitter Mickey Rivers watched as the trainer, Gene Monahan, examined the bruised toe. Then he presented Dent with his own bat instead of the one Bucky had used in the first swing. "I was ahead on the count after Bucky hit the foul ball off his foot," said Torrez. "I was trying to come inside and I got the ball out over the plate. He had this little chokeup swing. Other balls were hit out to left and were not going anywhere."

On this crisp, windy New England afternoon Torrez watched left fielder Carl Yastrzemski touch his glove and continue to drift back as the ball sailed his way.

"I could see flags showing a little breeze out there. The ball went right over the fence. I just stood on the mound and thought, 'Oh no.' I wasn't that upset about it. I was sure we would score a lot more runs," he said.

Thurman Munson doubled home a run and Reggie Jackson homered the next inning as the Yankees pushed the score to 5-2. Two Boston runs in the ninth inning off Goose Gossage only made it close.

Torrez was the loser in the now infamous "Bucky Dent game," as Bostonians recall it with an expletive.

"Yeah, I guess it's the thing most remembered about me," Torrez says some 25 years later. "I didn't lose any sleep over it."

Why should he?

Michael Augustine Torrez, born August 28, 1946, in Topeka, Kansas, had a sparkling big-league career over 18 seasons with St. Louis, Montreal, Baltimore, Oakland, the Yankees, the Red Sox, the New York Mets and a final couple of games with Oakland again in 1984.

He won 185 games against 160 losses, had a 3.97 ERA, struck out 1,404 batters and reached 20 wins in 1975 with Baltimore, the standard of pitching excellence.

He pitched two complete-game Series wins for the Yankees in his 1977 season in New York and beat the Dodgers twice. Everybody remembers the last game of that Series because Reggie hit three home runs.

"I won that game and caught the last out when Lee Lacy popped a bunt back to the mound and I waved everybody off to catch it," he said.

As a Mexican-American by birth who spoke fluent Spanish, Torrez may have saved the '77 season for the Yankees on a hot June 18 in Boston. The Yankees and Red Sox were playing a nationally televised game.

Jackson, whose heritage was part Spanish, was in right field when Jim Rice hit a short fly ball down the line. Jackson never got close to it as Rice raced to second with a double.

Manager Billy Martin, livid at what he saw as lack of hustle, sent Paul Blair to right field to replace Jackson. Jackson jogged to the bench, removed his glasses and confronted his manager.

"You show me up, and I'll show you up," Martin screamed.

"What did I do? What did I do?" Jackson asked.

Soon they were moving toward each other with venom in their eyes. Coaches Yogi Berra and Elston Howard kept them apart.

Torrez, not pitching in the game, spoke to Jackson in Spanish.

"I just told him to go inside, get away and go back to the hotel," Torrez said.

After the 10-4 Boston win, Torrez joined Jackson in his hotel room. They sat there together for several hours, speaking calmly, drinking a little wine, ordering room service and avoiding the press.

"By the next day," Torrez recalled, "Reggie had calmed down. He went on to have that great season and hit those three Series homers."

The Yankees won the Series with Martin as skipper that year and won again the next season after the combustible Martin resigned and a calm Bob Lemon took over.

"It was quite an exciting two years for me, for the Yankees, for the Red Sox and for all of baseball," Torrez laughed.

After he retired in 1984, Torrez chose to remain in the New York area. He opened a sports marketing business, living in White Plains with his family, playing a lot of golf at charity events and appearing often at banquets and card shows.

In February of 2003, Torrez and Dent, the parties of the first and second part in that historic playoff afternoon, were joined together in New York City at the annual banquet of the New York Baseball Writers Association.

"It's been 25 years since that happened," said Torrez. "It's amazing that people still make a big fuss about it. I guess they always will."

    Another famous twosome, Bobby Thomson and Ralph Branca, could relate. This pair were also connected by a playoff home run in 1951 and were often rejoined at public events, even 50 years later.

    "I guess we'll still be doing this in 2028 like Branca and Thomson," said Torrez.

    "I did a lot of good things in my career, but yeah, fans might say, 'He gave up the home run to Bucky'. Most fans will know I was a good pitcher. You could say it was a big home run," Torrez said.

    How big?

    How high is the moon?

BUCKY DENT

He entered the VIP hotel ballroom early on the evening of February 2, 2003, handsome in that perfect-fitting tuxedo, his hair thick and cut short, a little gray around the edges, his brown eyes sparkling, his smile wide and his manner as warm as ever.

Bucky Dent shook hands all around with welcoming sportswriters, with Yankee officials, with award winners, MVPs and Cy Young pitchers among them, and smiled for photographers.

They ganged up on him and Mike Torrez, the pitcher who threw that pitch on October 2, 1978, that cemented Dent's place in the game's history.

The baseball writers of New York had decided to honor Dent and Torrez in the 25th anniversary year of the playoff game won by the Yankees 5-4 after Dent's three-run homer put them ahead.

"I really can't imagine this happening," he said. "I guess it's hard to recognize that 25 years have gone by. I'm not kidding. To me it seems like it happened three or four years ago, as if I was still playing."

The homer made Dent a Yankee immortal. Though it hasn't earned him a plaque in Monument Park, it did make him a lasting villain in Boston baseball lore. His name is often spoken in late-night

NEW YORK YANKEES

BUCKY DENT

SHORTSTOP

SEASONS WITH YANKEES: 1977-82

Best Season with Yankees: 1980 (All-Star)

**Games: 141 • Batting Average: .262 • At-Bats: 489 • Hits: 128 •
Runs: 57 • Doubles: 26 • Home Runs: 5 • RBI: 52 • BB: 48 •
SO: 37**

Boston bar sermons around Fenway Park, rarely without an expletive added.

"I remember getting a lot of hate mail from Boston after it happened," he said. "People take their baseball seriously up there."

It was nothing like the hate mail Bill Buckner got after his 1986 World Series error on Mookie Wilson's grounder as the Mets kept the Red Sox from the World Series victory.

"With the passage of time it is more older fans, fathers, who come up to me with kids and say to them,

'This is the guy who…' I can tell sometimes they are from Boston by their accents. I just laugh," he said.

Russell Earl Dent—he was born Russell Earl O'Dey and adopted his mother's second husband's name—is from Savannah, Georgia. He was born November 25, 1951, and was playing ball early on.

"I was just one of those kids fascinated by sports. I always had a ball in my hand as far back as I can remember. I was a pretty good player in high school, and then the White Sox signed me for $10,000," he said.

Dent made it to Comiskey Park in 1973, became the regular Chicago shortstop for the next three seasons and was traded to the Yankees in 1977. The Yankees had won the pennant in 1976 without a real solid shortstop.

He fit in perfectly with the rowdy Yankee chemistry as one of the few quiet guys, batted an adequate .247 and .243 in the Series-winning years of 1977 and 1978.

The Yankees captured the imagination of New York City and the country with their performances in those two years. Dent, about as cute as a ballplayer could be with that toothpaste smile, and his first wife, Stormy, were instant celebrities after the homer and his World Series MVP performance in 1978 with a .417 average.

His career batting average was .247 over 12 years with the White Sox, Yankees, Texas and Kansas City. In the field, he was no Ozzie Smith (who is?) but he covered the ground, had good hands, made the double play and caused no clubhouse trouble.

"I had that hot streak in the Series," he remembered, "but I could always put the bat on the ball."

He was a good bunter, ran well, was a smart player and had that steady glove. It made for a nice career.

Dent always enjoyed teaching the game to youngsters and opened up a baseball school near his home in Boynton Beach, Florida.

High school and college players come through each year with hopes of improving their skills and reaching those million-dollar big-league salaries.

He managed in the Yankee minor league organization after his playing days ended. He even had a quick turn as Yankee manager when he replaced outspoken Dallas Green as the Yankee skipper in 1989 and was replaced the next season by ultimate loyalist Stump Merrill.

At least George always knew Dent's name. Steinbrenner called his successor Bump at his announcement press conference.

Those were the days prior to Joe Torre's reign when owner George Steinbrenner changed managers almost as often as he changed secretaries. In the earlier Steinbrenner days there was always Billy Martin, a five-time foil. After Martin's 1989 death in a car crash, Steinbrenner kept Dent around into 1990, shifted to Merrill, went with Buck Showalter and then settled on big-time winner Torre.

Dent's firing was one of the calmest in Steinbrenner's 30-plus years as Yankee boss. He accepted it as the gentleman he was, and Steinbrenner made sure he was paid properly for his efforts.

Dent coached for the Cardinals and the Texas Rangers after his Yankee managerial career ended, spent the 2002 season as manager of Kansas City's Omaha Royals Triple A club and accepted a post again in 2003 as manager of the Yankees top farm club in Columbus, Ohio.

"I really enjoy managing," he said. "I hope this leads to another opportunity in the big leagues as a manager, but if it doesn't, at least I'm still in the game."

He gets right back down to Florida after any baseball season ends so he can supervise his school and bring along some hopeful prospects for the game.

"It is tremendously satisfying to watch these kids improve after they spend time in our school," he said.

"I am sure one of these days we will have a kid who becomes a big-league star after playing with us."

As the Baseball Writers Dinner wore on in February of 2003 at the Sheraton Hotel in Manhattan, fans gathered around such stars as Barry Bonds, Randy Johnson and even old-timer guest Sandy Koufax for autographs.

A lot of them wanted Bucky Dent's autograph as well. They also wanted, in most cases, a chance to shake his hand, smile at him with their own memories of that October 1978 day and pose for pictures with the cutest guy on that famous team.

He may not be in Monument Park at the Stadium, but memories of Bucky Dent remain in a lot of heads and hearts around New York and Boston.

Where Have You Gone?

CHRIS CHAMBLISS

It was a chilly April afternoon in 2003 at Shea Stadium, home of the New York Mets, in Queens, New York.

The Cubs were in town to play the Mets with most interest centering around Chicago outfielder Sammy Sosa and his quest for his 500th career home run. The Mets were finishing batting practice before the game, and a husky right-handed pitcher walked off the mound.

Chris Chambliss came over to the dugout, shook hands with an old sportswriter pal and toweled himself off from his chores.

He works as the Mets minor league hitting coordinator with inspections and observations of all the teams in the Mets system, from nearby Brooklyn at KeySpan Park to faraway Kingsport, Tennessee.

He was helping out with the big club because hitting instructor Denny Walling had to undergo medical treatment for a damaged coronary artery.

"I'll be here for a while until Denny is ready to take over again," said Chambliss, the man who held the same job on the Mets in 2002 under manager Bobby Valentine.

Chambliss was born December 26, 1948, in Dayton, Ohio where his father served as a Navy chaplain.

NEW YORK YANKEES

CHRIS
CHAMBLISS

1st BASE

SEASONS WITH YANKEES: 1974-79; 1988

Best Season with Yankees: 1976 (All-Star; Finished fifth in MVP voting)

Games: 156 • **Batting Average: .293** • At-Bats: 641 (second in AL) • **Hits: 188 (third in AL)** • Runs: 79 • **Doubles: 32 (sixth in AL)** • Home Runs: 17 • **RBI: 96 (fourth in AL)** • Extra Base Hits: 55 (sixth in AL) • **Total Bases: 283 (second in AL)**

He played three seasons for the Indians before an emotional trade in 1974 brought him to the New York Yankees. Neither Chambliss nor the Yankee players on that team were too thrilled at the trade.

"It took some adjustment," he said. "After all this was New York and the Yankees."

He struggled his first season with the team and then established himself as a Yankee star in 1975 with a .304 average, 72 RBIs and a solid glove around first base.

On October 14, 1976, Chambliss became a legendary Yankee when he homered in the bottom of the ninth inning of the fifth and final ALCS game against Kansas City righthander Mark Littell. The blow gave the Yankees their 30th American League pennant and first in a dozen years.

He still hasn't touched home plate.

"There were just too many fans out there for me to get to the plate," he said. "I just circled around the bases and ran for the dugout."

After the Royals were retired in the top of the ninth of a tie game, the restless Yankee fans turned loud and rowdy in hopes of a title. They threw things on the field and screamed without stop. They forced the umpires to hold up the game as the field was cleaned.

Chambliss had his own special model bat, a C284 weighing 33 ounces and stretching 35 inches. In his hands he swung it over and over again before walking to the plate.

"I just told everybody on the bench after the delay that I would swing on the first pitch. Pitchers sometimes lose their concentration in an incident like that," he said.

Sure enough, the hard-throwing Littell grooved one for Chambliss, and he quickly deposited it into the right field seats for the pennant-winning homer.

"I still have the bat and the ball in my home," he said. "Some Stadium cop recovered it for me and brought it in after the game. I should have had him sign it to authorize it, but I never did. I guess people will just have to believe me."

Chambliss and his wife, Audra, a New York café lounge singer, have one son, Russell, who played a few years in the Yankee system before quitting for a teaching job. They make their home in West New York, New Jersey.

"You know, the thing about that hit is that every time I see it again on television I see something I didn't remember happening," he said.

He played on Yankee World Series winners in 1977 and 1978 against the Los Angeles Dodgers before moving on to Atlanta for seven seasons.

Chambliss managed in the Detroit and Atlanta organizations before coming back to the big leagues as a hitting instructor with Joe Torre's St. Louis Cardinals. He came back to the Yankees as the team's hitting coach in 1996 when Torre was selected by owner George Steinbrenner as the new manager.

He stayed there through the 2000 season where he collected four more World Series championship rings to go with the two he earned as a Yankee player.

Chambliss managed in the Florida Marlins organization and served as a Pittsburgh organization batting coach before the Mets brought him back to New York in 2002.

When new Mets manager Art Howe decided to go with his own man, Denny Walling, as the team's hitting coach, Chambliss was let go to seek other opportunities.

"I didn't get a single call for an interview for a big-league managerial job," he said. "That was disappointing."

Chambliss's former Yankee teammate, Willie Randolph, got most of the managerial interviews for minorities after the 2002 season ended.

"I still haven't given up," Chambliss said. "I think I have paid my dues in the minors. I am ready to manage in the big leagues as soon as somebody will take a chance on me."

Chambliss wasn't a very popular player when he first joined the Yankees in 1974 on a team filled with loud talkers and frequent complainers about the Boss, George Steinbrenner.

Chambliss just went out and did his job every day as a left-handed slugger and comfortable fielder. He was always a class act, a man of dedication and integrity, and someone who seemed unmoved in his performance by all the noise and turmoil around the Yankee organization.

"It's a long, long time, more than 27 years since I hit that home run," he said.

"The Yankees haven't marked it in any historical way as far as I know. As the years go by, those things tend to get forgotten."

Chambliss is still hopeful some big-league club will get smart enough to give him a chance at managing even though he isn't a Billy Martin type of "rah rah" skipper. But, a lot of quiet fellows, like his 1978 skipper Bob Lemon, also are successful in the World Series.

"Sure, I'd like the shot," he said, as he sat on the New York Mets bench at Shea Stadium. "I hope it comes. If not, I'm just happy being in the game and I hope I can help some kids."

Maybe one of them might even hit an historic home run for a pennant.

BOB
KUZAVA

He is seen on television every October during World Series time, that large number 21 on his Yankee uniform back, moving away from the charging second baseman Billy Martin, watching hopefully as Martin lunges for the popup first baseman Joe Collins never saw.

"If I didn't get out of the way," laughed Bob Kuzava, "Billy would have run me over."

Kuzava, a flame-throwing lefthander, was brought into the seventh game of the 1952 World Series against the Brooklyn Dodgers. Left-handed slugger Duke Snider was the Dodger hitter with the bases loaded.

Kuzava got Snider to pop up.

He then looked out at the Yankee bullpen in Ebbets Field. Righthander Johnny Sain was throwing. The next Dodger hitter was right-handed batter Jackie Robinson, one of the great clutch hitters of all time.

"Casey [Stengel] came to the mound. I was sure he would go with Sain against Jackie. Then Yogi [Berra] told Casey, 'He's throwin' good.' Casey said, 'All right, get 'em out.' Then he turned and walked away."

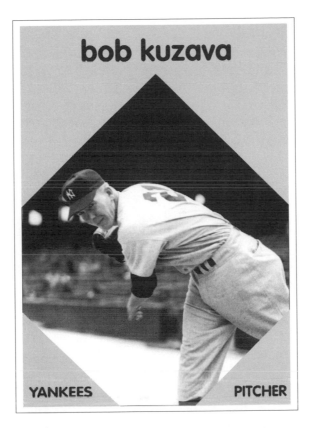

SEASONS WITH YANKEES: 1951-54

Best Season with Yankees: 1952

Games: 28 • Record: 8-8 • ERA: 3.45 • Innings Pitched: 133 •
Hits Allowed: 115 • Strikeouts: 67 • Walks: 63 • Complete
Games: 6 • Saves: 3

Kuzava ran the count to 3-2 against Robinson. He threw a high fastball just off the plate. Robinson got the end of the bat on the ball and popped it into the sun.

"Collins never moved and Yogi stood in front of home plate with his mask on. They weren't going to catch it. Then I saw Billy coming hard and I got out of the way," he said.

Martin caught the popup knee high a few feet from the mound for the third out. Kuzava retired the next six Dodgers to save the seventh game win and the Series.

Yankee players pounded Martin on the back as he came to the bench after the catch.

"Can you believe this?" Martin said to his young pal Mickey Mantle, who had hit a sixth inning homer to put the Yankees ahead. "They pat you on the back for catching a popup."

Stengel always bragged about the catch and decades later when he would spot Martin he would shout, "He made the catch on Robinson and you could look it up."

Kuzava was born May 28, 1923, in Wyandotte, Michigan where he still makes his home and watches all the baseball he can on television. He and his wife of 60 years, Dona ("The luckiest thing that ever happened to me," he said), are the parents of five children, grandparents of six and great grandparents of two.

"I played high school and American Legion ball and then I went into the service," Kuzava said. "When I came out the Indians signed me and I made the club. I went to the White Sox and then to Washington. Then in 1951 the Yankees traded for me," he said.

General manager George Weiss called Kuzava and told him he was going to start for the Yankees that Sunday.

"I told him I couldn't. I was on crutches. Nellie Fox had spiked me in the Achilles tendon on a play at first base. I thought they would kill the deal when he heard that," Kuzava said.

Weiss decided to wait it out. Kuzava took his family home to Michigan from Washington, waited a couple of weeks more and returned to New York. Stengel decided to use him mostly in relief until his ankle grew stronger.

"Most of my career in New York was like that, some starts, some relief. I did whatever they wanted," he said.

Kuzava could throw as hard as anybody in the game in his time, maybe in the middle 90s or high 90s on occasion, though they didn't have speed measuring guns in those days.

"I just think the good Lord gave me the ability to throw hard," said Kuzava, who stood six foot two and weighed more than 200 pounds at his peak. "A lot of the guys could run it up there like that: [Allie] Reynolds, [Vic] Raschi with us and [Bob] Feller, [Hal] Newhouser and [Mickey] McDermott around the league. I think the more you throw, the harder you throw."

Kuzava registered a 49-44 record in the big leagues over 10 seasons with 13 saves and two more in the 1951 and 1952 Yankee World Series wins over the Giants and Dodgers.

"I was with a lot of different teams in my career, but you know what? I only think of myself as a Yankee. Once a Yankee, always a Yankee," he said.

He lived near Yankee Stadium in the town of Ridgewood, New Jersey during his days as a Yankee and can still recall the laughs he had driving to the ballpark every day in a car pool with Mantle, Gene Woodling and Gil McDougald.

"We never talked about the game. We talked about everything else," he said. "Mantle could just be hysterical in telling stories."

Kuzava's top salary in baseball was $19,000 a year but he hardly cared.

"I could buy a beautiful house out here in Wyandotte for $12,000 and I could buy the best car around for $2,000. That wasn't so bad. Now they have a kid like this [Alex] Rodriguez making $22 million. At least he's the best player in the game. I remember once I was holding out for a few hundred more. George Weiss said to me, 'Have a nice summer in Wyandotte.' That made me sign real fast," he said.

Kuzava scouted for a few years after leaving the game but only made a few thousand dollars, not enough to support his large family.

"I just came home and got a job in the beer business. I would go all over in the area and make sales. I did a lot better than baseball in that. Once in a while I would even drive the truck and haul those barrels into the stores. It kept me in shape, and I made a nice living at it," he said.

Kuzava retired from the beer business when he was 58 years old. Now, at the age of 80, he enjoys telling baseball stories to his grandchildren, playing a little golf and watching baseball on television.

"It was just great being a Yankee. It was all about winning. I remember one time a kid joined us and didn't run out a ground ball. Hank Bauer got him in the dugout and asked, 'Are you tired?' The guy never dogged it after that. They were fooling with our Series money," he said.

Kuzava made it to three World Series with the Yankees but has a special fondness watching that 1952 classic with Martin making the catch every year on the Robinson popup.

"Every once in a while I catch it on Classic Sports Network, the entire game," he said. "I just laugh when I see myself backing away from the ball to let Billy be a hero."

MOOSE
SKOWRON

O nly Yogi Berra can compete with Moose Skowron for the title of most popular face of any former Yankee.

See, it is all about the haircut—that tight crewcut circa 1950 on a guy looks a little amusing and so much thinner now on a guy who still appears tough and strong in his 70s.

Then there is the name. William Joseph Skowron—born December 18, 1930, in Chicago, Illinois—became "Moose" as a young Chicago street kid and rode it to fame and some modest baseball fortune over 14 years in the big leagues.

"This was during World War II," said Skowron, while on a summer visit to New York for another baseball card show. "The kids were playing in the streets, just running around, and I had that tight crewcut and probably looked a little bald."

One youngster called young Billy Skowron "Mussolini," and the other kids all laughed. They thought the bulky youngster with the tight crewcut looked like the Italian World War II leader, Benito Mussolini.

"It was just a kid thing and all of a sudden they were all calling me 'Mussolini, Mussolini' and then it just became 'Moose.' That stuck," he said.

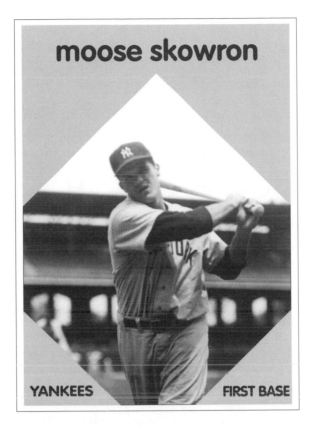

moose skowron

YANKEES   FIRST BASE

SEASONS WITH YANKEES: 1954-62

Best Season with Yankees: 1960 (All-Star; Finished ninth in MVP voting)

Games: 146 • Batting Average: .309 (fourth in AL) • At-Bats: 538 • Hits: 166 (seventh in AL) • Runs: 63 • Doubles: 34 (second in AL) • Home Runs: 26 (eighth in AL) • RBI: 91 (eighth in AL) • Extra Base Hits: 63 (second in AL) • Total Bases: 284 (third in AL) • Slugging Percentage: .528 (fifth in AL)

Skowron moved rapidly through an impressive high school and Purdue University career as a football and baseball star and arrived with Casey Stengel's Yankees in 1954.

"I had played some outfield and pitched a little. I could always hit, so I had a chance to make the club. They didn't have the DH in those days so I had to find a position. I wasn't fast enough for the outfield so Casey thought I could play first base."

After a few workouts that spring of 1954, Skowron made the club as a backup to Joe Collins, the left-handed-hitting first baseman. Skowron, a righthander all the way, had to learn how to play the position comfortably before he could settle in.

"One day Casey pulled me aside and said I needed help with my footwork. He said I was getting all twisted up at first base, and if I didn't learn how to play the position I wouldn't be around very long," Skowron said.

He was dispatched to an Arthur Murray Dance Studio in the Bronx near Yankee Stadium. While others were learning the fox trot, the tango and the cha cha, Skowron was learning to put one foot next to the other without getting them twisted.

"The girl that ran the place knew I had been sent over by the Yankees, and she gave me a little extra time before the class and afterwards. I did all the regular steps during the one-hour lessons," he said.

In a few weeks the husky athlete was learning to be light on his feet. All of it played out well as Skowron became an excellent first baseman with a great pair of hands.

"My hands were big and strong," he said. "Even though I didn't run well I could cover enough ground at first base and if I got to the ball I would always make the play."

His rookie season of 1954 was a tough one for Skowron with the Yankees even though he batted .340 in 87 games.

In Stengel's 12 seasons he won more than 100 ball games only once, in that 1954 season. It so happened the Indians won a record 111 games that year and beat the Yankees out of the pennant, the first Yankee loss in Stengel's time, by eight games.

"Casey was pretty grouchy that season even though we were winning. He had won five in a row and wanted another one. I learned a lot about the Yankees. Even though I was hitting the ball well, it didn't matter. It was all about winning the title," Skowron said.

Skowron showed good power to all fields as a strong line drive hitter. He also hit a lot of balls that were caught in deep left center field.

"Casey just knew so much about the game and so much about each and every player. He could quickly see that I wasn't going to be a home run hitter or maybe even a high average hitter if I concentrated on pulling the ball," Skowron said.

Skowron had to learn how to take advantage of the short right field wall in Yankee Stadium and direct more of his drives that way.

"I spent a lot of hours out there hitting line drives to right field. I became pretty good at it to the point where I could wait on a pitch and even drive an inside pitch to the right field corner," he said.

It probably took the pitchers around the American League a half-dozen years before they realized Skowron was one of the strongest right-handed hitters in the game with enormous power to the right side of the field.

"There were times I would get a surprised look from the pitcher when I drove his high outside waste pitch over the wall in right. That was just a little shot for me but it counted," he said.

Skowron put together four .300 seasons in a row from 1954 through 1957 with three pennant-winning years and two World Series victories in that time.

"We may not have had the best personnel every year, but Casey really knew how to use guys. He rested me against certain right-handed pitchers and he used [Hank] Bauer and [Gene] Woodling in ways that made them mad but made them more productive. I think Hank even admits today that it lengthened his career," Skowron said.

Skowron recorded his best season in Stengel's final year with the Yankees in 1960. He batted .309 in 146 games, slugged 26 homers and knocked in 91 runs.

"That was a great season until the World Series," Skowron said. "I still can't believe we didn't win."

That was the year Pittsburgh defeated the Yankees four games to three. Skowron hit .375 in seven games, had a dozen hits, hit a couple of home runs, scored seven runs and knocked in half a dozen.

"I was just standing there on first base when [Ralph] Terry threw that pitch that [Bill] Mazeroski hit over the wall for the winning run. That was about as low a feeling as I ever had in baseball," he said.

He won two more pennants and another World Series in the famous Maris-Mantle home run year of 1961 before his Yankee career was ended in November of 1962 with a trade to Los Angeles for right-handed pitcher Stan Williams.

"I wanted to finish my career with the Yankees. That trade was really a blow for me. At least I was able to go to a good club and got back into the World Series that next season with a great Dodger club— [Sandy] Koufax, [Don] Drysdale, [Johnny] Podres and those other great pitchers. We swept the Yankees in the Series but every game was low scoring and close," he said.

Skowron finished up with Washington, the Chicago White Sox and the California Angels after the 1967 season.

He batted .282 in 14 seasons with eight World Series appearances and six championship rings.

"I played for a few other clubs, but I never really considered myself anything but a Yankee," Skowron said. "That's where it all started for me and that's what I tell people now when I sign at these shows. I'm a Yankee."

Skowron spent some time in sales with a couple of trucking and warehousing outfits after his playing days ended and still makes his home in the Chicago area in the town of Schaumburg. He and his wife Lorraine have three children.

"I enjoy playing golf at these tournaments like the one for the Roger Maris charities in Fargo, North Dakota, and a few I get invited to back east," he said.

Skowron said he still follows baseball and spends time telling his children and grandchildren about his playing days in the big leagues, mostly with the Yankees.

"I look forward to the card shows when the guys get together, and I certainly look forward to being invited back to the Stadium for an Old Timers game. That's still a big kick for me walking into that clubhouse and going back on the field," he said.

Even now, about half a century after he first came to New York as an awkward first baseman with a funny haircut, Skowron is as popular a former Yankee as there is around.

The fans always yell "Moose" when he takes the field, and they don't mean current pitcher Mike Mussina.

JOHNNY BLANCHARD

I t was May 3, 1965, and manager Johnny Keane of the Yankees, who had defeated the New York team in the World Series as St. Louis Cardinals skipper a few months earlier, called catcher John Blanchard into his office.

"We've traded you to Kansas City. Good luck," said Keane.

Then he dismissed Blanchard and gave the same trade news to pitcher Rollie Sheldon. Both Yankees were traded to Kansas City that day for highly regarded catcher Doc Edwards.

Edwards hit all of .190 in 45 games for New York before moving on. It was maybe the worst Yankee trade ever.

"That was a very sad, tough day for me," Blanchard said. "It just hurt so much."

Blanchard had been in the Yankee organization more than 10 years by then, a vital player in a backup role on the 1961 Yankees, the Maris-Mantle home run year team and a Yankee club considered by many even better than the famed 1927 Yankees.

When Keane informed Blanchard about the trade, the catcher-pinch hitter walked to his locker, sat down for an instant and burst into tears.

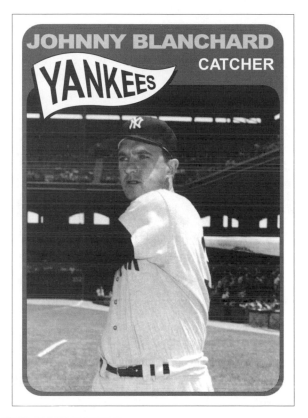

SEASONS WITH YANKEES: 1955; 1959-65

Best Season with Yankees: 1961

Games: 93 • Batting Average: .305 • At-Bats: 243 •
Hits: 74 • Runs: 38 • Home Runs: 21 • RBI: 54 •
Slugging Percentage: .613

As teammates walked by to console him and wish him well and reporters begged for his verbal reactions to the deal, Blanchard filled the Yankee clubhouse with gasps and tears.

Photographers were allowed inside the Yankee clubhouse in those days—a press privilege no longer granted to the inquiring media—and newspapers the next day filled their sports pages with shots of Blanchard, wrapped in a towel, his head down on his hands, bawling like a baby.

It was just about the most emotional reaction to a trade away from the Yankees anybody around the clubhouse that day had ever seen.

A reporter tried to console Blanchard with the realistic observation that after so many years as a backup to Yogi Berra and Elston Howard, he would finally get an opportunity to be an every-day catcher.

"That doesn't matter," he finally said that day. "It won't be with the Yankees."

The deal took the desire for playing out of Blanchard's heart. The happy-go-lucky Yankee backup catcher and occasional pinch hitter became an unhappy, dour, disappointed player with Kansas City and Milwaukee.

Blanchard played only 52 games with Kansas City and another 10 with Milwaukee before deciding to go home to Minnesota. He was 32 years old when he quit baseball.

"I wasn't a Yankee any more," he said.

John Edwin Blanchard was born in Minneapolis on February 26, 1933. He was signed by the Yankees after an outstanding high school career and joined the team at the end of 1955 before coming back to stay with the big club in 1959.

Future Hall of Famer Yogi Berra was nearing the end of his playing days but Elston Howard was at his peak when Blanchard came to the team.

He was a left-handed slugger with right field home run power in the Stadium and hit as many as 21 homers in 93 games in the amazing 1961 season. He had a career total of 67 homers in 1,193 at bats, a notable 17.8 at bats-per-home run ratio.

That 1961 season was the year Maris hit a new record 61 homers, Mantle had 54 and Berra, Howard and Blanchard hit 64 home runs among them.

Berra often kidded Maris and Mantle by saying, "Us catchers hit more than either of you did."

Howard hit .348 that year, Mantle hit .317 and Blanchard batted .305 in the best year of his career.

"That was just a wonderful season," Blanchard said. "Roger and Mickey were having those remarkable home run years, and it was just fun to be part of that team. There were a lot of days when I would get a big hit and maybe win a game and the press still ganged up on Roger."

Blanchard, who stood six foot one and weighed 193 pounds at his peak, was an adequate if unspectacular catcher with a strong arm. He called a good game and he was a tough guy around home plate when any runner thought he could score.

"I enjoyed catching and I enjoyed calling the game," he said. "There weren't too many pitchers on the Yankees who would ever shake me off."

Blanchard went home to his wife, Nancy, and their three children, accepted a job in sales for a Minnesota firm and traveled throughout the state for several years.

He retired in his late 50s due to ill health, played a lot of golf and hit most of the 10,000 lakes in Minnesota with his fishing pole.

"The most fun I have these days outside of the family is going to a baseball card show and spending time with the other guys," he said. "When I get invited back to Yankee Stadium now it looks a lot different from my time. But I know it is still the Stadium, and the Yankees still play there. It makes it all worthwhile."

He spends a lot of time with old teammates Hank Bauer and Bill Skowron.

"We just have so many laughs when we are together reliving a lot of the good times," he said. "When you get older it is just so much fun to share the stories of the old days."

He turned 70 years old in 2003 but Blanchard appeared healthy and strong at a Yankee Old Timers Day reunion.

"There is just something about walking into this clubhouse that makes you feel young again," he said. "I look at all these kids in here [the current Yankees] and I think back to my own time. There is just nothing like playing for the Yankees. I feel sorry for guys who never made it here," he said.

His career spanned eight years in the big-leagues and featured 516 games, five straight World Series appearances from 1960 to 1964 (in which he sported a .345 Series average) and one horrible trade.

He gets a little choked up when he is asked about that May day in 1965 even now.

"I always wanted to be a Yankee when I was growing up," he said. "That is all I ever wanted to be."

He certainly showed how much that meant to him when they took his pinstripes away.

ALLIE
CLARK

He was a backup outfielder to guys named Joe DiMaggio, Tommy Henrich and Charlie Keller during the 1947 season and he pinch hit in the World Series that year for a rookie named Yogi Berra.

Allie Clark had only 67 at-bats for the Yankees in his seven-year career that included another World Series in 1948 with Cleveland and some playing time with the Philadelphia A's and the Chicago White Sox.

Like all of them, he is most fond of his time as a Yankee in Yankee Stadium.

"I have lived around New Jersey all my life," said Clark, a native and resident still of South Amboy, New Jersey. He was born in that town on June 16, 1923.

"I would see the guys who lived in this area and played with the Yankees every so often. I was real close to Joe Collins and I would run into Yogi every so often at a sports banquet or at a golf outing. A lot of people don't think he was ever [pinch] hit for in baseball."

Manager Bucky Harris sent Clark up to hit for Berra, a little overwhelmed in his first Series with a .158 average, against Brooklyn lefthander Joe Hatten in the 1947 classic. Clark, a right-handed batter, slapped a single to left in the 5-2 Yankee seventh-game win.

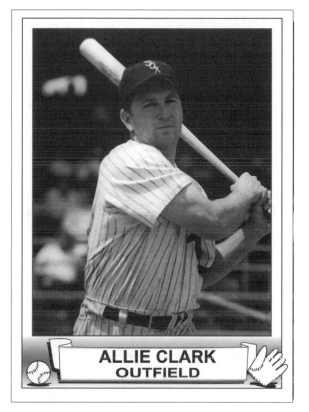

ALLIE CLARK
OUTFIELD

SEASONS WITH YANKEES: 1947

Best Season with Yankees: 1947

Games: 24 • **Batting Average:** .373 • At-Bats: 67 • **Hits: 25** •
Runs: 9 • **Home Runs: 1** • RBI: 14

"I ran into one of Yogi's kids at some banquet and told him I had batted for his father in the World Series. 'Nah, that didn't happen.' I told him it did happen. He could go home and look up the box score. There it was. Clark batted for Berra. The box scores don't lie," Clark said.

Alfred Aloysius Clark was signed by the Yankees in 1941 out of St. Mary's of South Amboy High School.

"It's just a small place, but it turned out at least five big-leaguers, including myself, Tom Kelly, who managed Minnesota for a long time and the O'Brien twins, Eddie and Johnny who played for Pittsburgh. That's quite an accomplishment," he said.

"My career was interrupted by the war. I served three years in Europe and then I came back January 1, 1946. I was in spring training with the Yankees that year with Yogi and Bobby Brown. We went down to the Newark club, and I made the Yankees in 1947," he said.

Clark batted a sparkling .373 in 24 games. He was traded to Cleveland the next year for a strong right-handed pitcher named Red Embree.

He was on that wonderful Cleveland team that featured playing manager Lou Boudreau that beat the Boston Braves in the 1948 playoffs.

"Two winning World Series teams in my first two years," he said.

"That wasn't a bad way to start a career."

Clark lost playing time with the Indians in the next couple of years and was traded to the A's in 1951. He finished with the White Sox and ended his seven-year big-league career with a .262 batting average.

"I never made any money ($11,000 was his highest salary), so in 1954 I just decided to quit. I had a lot of kids to support and I needed to do better financially. In those days, unless you were like [Joe] DiMaggio or [Ted] Williams you couldn't support a family on just a baseball salary. I wonder if these guys making the millions today ever heard of that."

As a youngster in South Amboy, Clark put in some part-time work as an iron worker on buildings, ships and bridges.

"I did that in the winters when I was playing ball. I had to make money outside or we couldn't get by. You ask any old time ballplayer and they will tell you about their jobs, working in stores, driving trucks, stocking stuff in warehouses, anything to support their families," he said.

When he went home in 1954 he became a full-time iron worker.

"It was good, steady work, outdoors and I always enjoyed it. I was a strong guy [six feet and 195 pounds in his playing days], and it didn't bother me. The guys were always fun. Once in a while they would kid me about being with the Yankees and ask me about Yogi. 'Did he really say those things?' We did important work, and I had a good time. Just like baseball," he said.

Clark and his wife Frances raised six children, have 14 grandchildren and eight great grandchildren.

"Most of them live in the area so we still have a lot of family events. I see them and I also go fishing a lot and even do a little crabbing around the shore," he said.

Clark said he has had some tough times with his health as he moved into his 80s.

"I had a five-way bypass a few years back, and then I was hit with a couple of cancers," he said.

"The doctors did a good job and got them out and kept me going. I can still relax at home, watch baseball, talk to the kids on the phone, read the papers and root for the Yankees. Yeah, I still do."

He didn't spend a lot of time with the Yankees, only 24 games' worth in 1947, but he considers it quality time. That 1947 Yankees World Series ring is the one he cherishes.

WILLIE RANDOLPH

O n an early spring afternoon in 2003, Willie Randolph, the Yankees' third base coach, pitched 20 minutes of batting practice under a warm sun.

He wiped the sweat off his face with a Yankee towel as he sat in the dugout while the players and other coaches relaxed inside the clubhouse at Yankee Stadium.

"I still get a kick just being out here," said Randolph, as he waved toward the deep outfield stands at the Bronx ballpark.

"This place is special for me, and no matter what happens it always will be."

Randolph had traveled around the country the previous winter as he was being interviewed for possible managerial jobs after being a coach with the Yankees since 1993.

"I think the interview with the Mets was just a sham, but I really thought I had a serious chance in Detroit and Milwaukee," he said. "Milwaukee was the closest I came. [Milwaukee GM] Doug Melvin was an old teammate, and we had a great interview. It just went the other way."

The Mets selected Art Howe as their manager after they interviewed Randolph and couldn't make a deal for Lou Piniella who wound

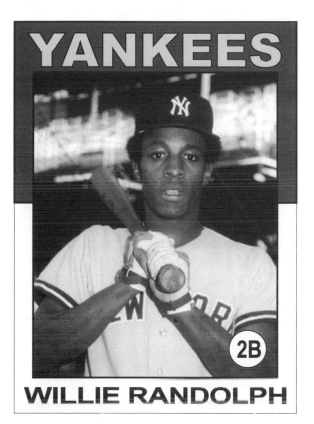

YANKEES

WILLIE RANDOLPH

2B

SEASONS WITH YANKEES: 1976-88

Best Season with Yankees: 1980 (All-Star)

Games: 138 • **Batting Average**: .294 • At-Bats: 513 • **Hits**: 151 • **Walks**: 119 (first in AL) • **Strikeouts**: 45 • Runs: 99 (ninth in AL) • **Home Runs**: 7 • RBI: 46 • **On-Base Percentage**: 427 (second in AL) • Stolen Bases: 30 (eighth in AL)

up in Tampa. Detroit picked old Tigers favorite Alan Trammell, and Milwaukee named Ed Yost as their manager in 2003.

"I think some teams gave me the run around just to deal with that minority hiring question but some teams were serious," Randolph said. "I still think it will happen."

Some anonymous sources claimed Randolph was not picked by at least two teams because of what was described as his "Yankee arrogance." He is entitled to it.

Randolph first became a Yankee in a trade with Pittsburgh on December 11, 1975 in a deal involving pitcher Doc Medich.

"That was certainly a dream come true for me and my family," said Randolph.

He was born in Holly Hill, South Carolina on July 6, 1954. His family soon moved to Brooklyn, New York where Randolph grew up on the mean streets of the Brownsville section of the New York City borough.

He was selected by the Pittsburgh Pirates in the 1972 free agent draft out of Brooklyn's Tilden High School and made it to the Pirates for 30 games in the 1975 season before moving on to the Stadium.

He batted .267 with the pennant-winning Yankees of 1976 (swept by the Big Red Machine of Cincinnati in the World Series) and anchored the 1977 World Series champions as Billy Martin's second baseman. He batted .274 that year.

"The most emotional baseball experience for me occurred that year of 1977 in the All-Star game. I was 23 years old and I was starting the game. I looked around that clubhouse and out on the field and all those great players, future Hall of Famers, (Rod) Carew, (Tom) Seaver, (Jim) Palmer, (Don) Sutton, (George) Brett were all out there with me. My family was in the stands, maybe 20, 30 people from Brooklyn and they were cheering me on. It was just something I could never forget."

Randolph made six All-Star appearances as a player and has added another half-dozen as a Yankee coach. He would like that first one as a big-eague manager.

"I'm still a young man. I know there is plenty of time. I'll be ready when they call," he said.

Randolph put in 18 big-league seasons with the Yankees, the Los Angeles Dodgers, Oakland A's and the Mets with a .276 career average and one of the finest gloves seen around the game. He also was named co-captain of the Yankees along with Ron Guidry in 1986.

He was on four Yankee World Series teams (he missed the 1978 Series with an injury) and played for Oakland in the 1990 Series against Cincinnati.

When he joined the Yankees for the 1976 season, new manager Billy Martin, who had played second base in his own playing time, filled Randolph with a lot of confidence.

"Billy helped me a lot," Randolph recalled. "He knew a lot about positioning and he knew an awful lot about how the game should be played."

That 1976 Yankees team was the first to win a pennant in a dozen years. It had so many talented players such as Thurman Munson, Lou Piniella, Roy White and Chris Chambliss, a deep pitching staff and an aggressive style of play typical of Billy Martin teams.

"The guys were really together," said Randolph. "I think Kansas City was just as good as we were, but we seemed to get the big hits when we needed them."

That team got into the unfortunate World Series against the powerful Reds on Chris Chambliss's famous home run against the Kansas City Royals. Cincinnati won all four games in the Series, though.

Owner George Steinbrenner thought the Yankees were a player short and signed Reggie Jackson, who later described himself in a magazine article as "the straw that stirs the drink."

Munson, Piniella, Randolph and the rest didn't take too warmly to that remark. Munson was the team captain, and tension could be cut with a butter knife around the Yankee clubhouse in those days.

While Jackson, Munson, Piniella, Catfish Hunter, Sparky Lyle and several others made their feelings known to the press all summer, Randolph quietly kept about his job of playing well, leading the team by example and commenting carefully.

It gained him much private and public respect, the kind of standing that should bode well in his future managerial career.

He showed more leadership qualities with the winning Dodgers and Oakland teams, had his finest batting year with Milwaukee at age 37 with a .327 mark in 124 games and added maturity to the Mets in his one season at Shea.

He soon rejoined the Yankees in the front office and then moved back on the field. He and his wife, Gretchen, have four children and have made their home for many years close to Yankee Stadium in nearby Franklin Lakes, New Jersey.

The young second baseman of the middle 1970s was a fine baseball player with a tough exterior and a sour side.

The coach of the 1990s and the 21st century is an intelligent, mature, self-confident, warm individual with incredible knowledge of the game.

The team that eventually selects Randolph as a manager won't be doing it to satisfy Commissioner Bud Selig's minority hiring demands. They will be doing it to satisfy their needs for a potential commanding manager.

ROY WHITE

I t was a ground-ball single, so familiar to Yankee fans, common among the 1,803 hits Roy White collected in 15 seasons in Yankee pinstripes.

"He would always do that," said teammate Lou Piniella. "Roy would get an important hit in the middle of an inning when somebody else would get the dramatic one."

This was on October 2, 1978, in Boston's Fenway Park, in one of the most famous games ever played in the 101 seasons of Yankee baseball.

The Yankees had driven relentlessly against the rest of the league and especially against Boston, catching them from 14 games behind. They had lost on the final Sunday of the season behind, of all people, future Hall of Famer Catfish Hunter.

Now they were in Boston for the playoff, the winner to face Kansas City in the American League Championship Series for the 1978 American League pennant. Bob Lemon had taken over for embattled Billy Martin as field leader of the Yankees and brought calm to a boiling inferno.

"I remember the playoff game atmosphere as pretty routine for us," recalled White. "We seemed to approach every game the same

SEASONS WITH YANKEES: 1965-79

Best Season with Yankees: 1970 (All-Star)

Games: 162 (first in AL) • **Batting Average: .296** • At-Bats: 609 (10th in AL) • **Hits: 180 (fifth in AL)** • Walks: 95 (eighth in AL) • **Strikeouts: 66** • Runs: 109 (third in AL) • **Doubles: 30** • Home Runs: 22 • **RBI: 94 (10th in AL)** • Stolen Bases: 24 (ninth in AL) • **Total Bases: 288 (sixth in AL)**

way. We had confidence without cockiness. We knew what we had to do. We also had [Ron] Guidry going for us."

Guidry was simply the best pitcher in baseball that year so the Yankees moved smoothly through batting practice and into the game with a sense of success in their minds. Boston led 2-0 into the top of the seventh with Mike Torrez pitching for them against the Yankee lefthander.

Graig Nettles started the seventh with a fly out. Chris Chambliss, who had won the pennant with one swing against Kansas City two years earlier, singled to right. White came to the plate.

He stood five foot 10, weighed 160 pounds, choked up on the bat a little from the left side of the plate as a switch hitter, looked at a couple of pitches for a 1-1 count and then slapped a ground ball past the pitcher, past second base and out into centerfield. He was on first with a hit, the tying run in the biggest game of his career.

Jim Spencer flied out for Brian Doyle as a lefty pinch hitter. Bucky Dent was next, and he hit that famous Fenway homer for a 3-2 Yankee lead on the way to a 5-4 playoff win.

"When I shook Bucky's hand at home plate I knew we would win. We had Guidry out there for us and Goose [Gossage] ready to come in. That's just the way it worked out," White said.

When it was over, when the Yankees had broken Boston's heart again, White sat quietly in a corner of the steamy, crowded clubhouse. The press ganged up on Dent, on Guidry, on Gossage, who popped up future Hall of Famer Carl Yastrzemski to close out the game, on manager Lemon, on owner George Steinbrenner, on GM Al Rosen, on anybody in the Yankee scene who was not Roy White.

"I never minded that," White said of his matter-of-fact acceptance. "I think playing with so many high profile players just made it easy for me."

Roy Hilton White—no relation to the hotel family—was born in Los Angeles on December 27, 1943. He was a small youngster who grew into a small man physically. He was good at sports from the start with a grace and confidence in his play.

The Yankees tried him as an infielder, and he made it to the Bronx in 1965. His teammates included Mickey Mantle, Elston Howard, Whitey Ford, and Roger Maris—unfortunately all in their declining seasons—under first-year Yankee skipper Johnny Keane.

White was a second baseman with good range but a weak arm. He was a switch hitter on a team with the greatest switch hitter ever, the powerful Mantle.

"I think people expected I would hit a lot of homers because I was a switch hitter," White said. "That was a factor in my slow early progress."

Keane, overwhelmed by the Yankee scene, at least understood White. He had some small outfielders with his great St. Louis Cardinals team and immediately got White into the Yankee outfield. He could catch anything in his area, but a weak arm undermined his overall play.

Soon, White's steady batting, his ability to hit good pitching, his wonderful eye at the plate, wonderful base-running skills and his astute sense of the game impressed all around the Yankees. He batted .267 with 17 homers in 1968 and then hit .290, .296 and .292 in his next three seasons.

He was established in the early 1970s as a rock-solid leadoff man or number-two batter. He was an every day player with few weaknesses and a determined winner on a team showing improvement almost every season after Steinbrenner brought the club from disinterested Columbia Broadcasting System in 1973 for $10 million. The Yankees of today may be worth, oh, maybe a billion.

"I saw that George would go out and spend money," said White. "When he outbid everybody for Catfish for 1975 we were on our way."

The Yankees won their first pennant in 12 seasons in 1976 and their first World Series in 1977 after 15 seasons. White, of course, was a vital if unspectacular player on those clubs.

He batted .269 in the comeback season of 1978 and slipped to .215 in his final year as a Yankee in 1979.

With a little urging from the Yankees, White moved on to play three seasons of productive baseball in Japan. He returned home with the promise of a job in the Yankee organization.

White served as a scout, worked in the front office, moved around the minor league organization and came to spring training each March as an instructor.

White and his wife, Linda, maintained their home in New Jersey with their two children as he stayed connected with the Yankees.

He was in several private sales businesses, made many appearances and was always available for autograph shows where fans appreciated his gentle kindness and his link to Yankee greatness.

In 2000 he was signed as a scout for the Oakland A's organization but nursed a dream that hinged on former teammate Willie Randolph's big-league managerial potential.

"Willie said that I would be the first coach he would sign as soon as he was named a manager," said White. "I just can't wait for that. It might even happen with the Yankees."

In the meantime, he remains in the game he loves with the same dignity, dedication and desire he always showed on the field. Other names get more attention. No names get more respect.

Roy White's dream was realized when he was named the first base coach of the Yankees in 2004.

JOHNNY
KUCKS

Yankees starter Don Larsen pitched the only World Series perfect game against the Brooklyn Dodgers in Game 5 of the 1956 Series.

Clem Labine, a Brooklyn relief pitcher, had started Game 6 in a surprise and had come up with another Series gem, a 10-inning seven-hit shutout in a 1-0 victory over Yankee fireballer Bob Turley.

Now the Series was tied at three games each, and Brooklyn had a rested Don Newcombe for Game 7 at Brooklyn's Ebbets Field against, well…manager Casey Stengel wasn't naming his starter.

"It was Game 7 and everybody was ready," said Johnny Kucks. "When you get down to the last game you don't have to save anybody."

Kucks, an 18-game winner that year in his second season with the Yankees, had relieved in the first two Series games, a 6-3 Brooklyn win in the Ebbets Field opener and a 13-8 Dodgers triumph in the second game.

It was October 10, 1956, when Kucks drove up to Yankee Stadium from his New Jersey home and boarded the bus with his teammates for the 30-minute ride to Brooklyn's Ebbets Field. It would be an historic date for a reason none of the participants could then recognize.

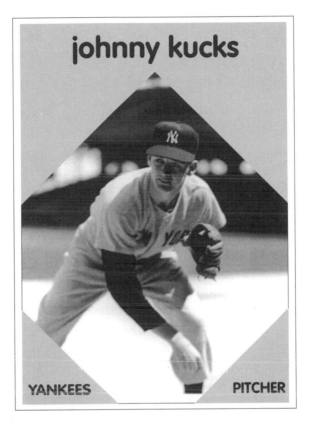

SEASONS WITH YANKEES: 1955-59

Best Season with Yankees: 1956 (All-Star)

Games: 34 • Record: 18-9 (ninth in AL in wins; seventh in AL in won-loss percentage) • ERA: 3.85 • Innings Pitched: 224 1/3 • Hits Allowed: 223 • Strikeouts: 67 • Walks: 72 • Complete Games: 12 • Shutouts: 3 (seventh in AL)

That afternoon would turn out to be the final World Series game ever played at historic Ebbets Field in the Flatbush section of Brooklyn. The Dodgers finished their time in Brooklyn in 1957 with a second-place finish and soon moved to Los Angeles.

"I got to the ballpark in Brooklyn, dressed and walked out on the field for a light pregame workout. I still didn't know if I was pitching or not," Kucks said.

He came into the visiting clubhouse to change his uniform shirt ("There wasn't much sweat on it," he remembered) and looked down at his game shoes. A shiny new baseball was in his right shoe, placed there by Yankee coach Frank Crosetti, who dated his time with the team back to 1932.

That was the signal Stengel used to advise a pitcher about his start that day.

"I was strong, I was rested and I was really confident we would score runs off Newcombe. We had hit him hard in his previous start," said Kucks.

When he went out to warm up on the field near home plate, as was the tradition in those Brooklyn days, Stengel also sent two other starting pitchers, Whitey Ford and Sturdivant, down under the stands.

"That didn't inspire me with confidence," admitted Kucks. "But that was Casey's way. He wasn't worried about your psyche. He was concerned with your performance."

Kucks had two runners on with Jackie Robinson at bat in the first inning. He looked down at the bullpen and saw Ford, the lefthander, and Sturdivant, a righty, warming up.

"I got Robinson to bounce into a double play and that eased things all around," Kucks said.

Kucks's performance was merely superb. He allowed the Dodgers only three hits while Yogi Berra hit two home runs, Elston Howard slugged another and Moose Skowron collected a grand slam.

Kucks coasted to a 9-0 Series victory in the final game for the 1956 championship.

"I guess Tom and Whitey got a little throwing in so they would be ready for the next season," Kucks said.

John Charles Kucks, six foot three and 170 pounds at his pitching peak, was born July 27, 1932, in Hoboken, New Jersey.

He pitched for several amateur teams around New Jersey before being signed by the Yankees out of Dickinson High in Jersey City in 1950.

He spent a couple of years in the minors, served in the Army in 1953 and 1954 and made it to the big-league club in 1955. He was helped by a rule in place in those days that allowed clubs to carry an extra two men if they had recently returned from service. Kucks and Billy Martin made the team in 1955 without being charged against the 25-man roster.

He worked as a starter and reliever, won eight games for the Yankees that year and got into two World Series games in relief against the Dodgers. The 1955 Dodgers actually beat the Yankees that October for the only Brooklyn championship.

Kucks had worked hard to develop a breaking pitch to go with his fastball in the spring of 1956. Pitching coach Jim Turner had improved his motion, his control and his breaking pitches.

"I really felt strong and confident going into that season," Kucks recalled. "We had a lot of pitching, but I thought I could win a job and fit in well as a starter."

He certainly did with 31 starts, 224 innings pitched and a sparkling 18-9 record. Only future Hall of Famer Whitey Ford won more games for that team with 19 victories.

"Ford started the Series for us and Casey went to Larsen for the second game. I was a little disappointed, especially when we lost the first two games. But Whitey came back to win the third game," he said.

Sturdivant won the fourth game, Larsen pitched his Series perfect game, Turley lost to Labine in Game 6 and Kucks was set for the closer.

"Even after all these years I still get people coming up to me asking about that game. It was really a special event in Yankee history," he said.

Kucks won eight games for the Yankees in 1957 and 1958 and then was traded to Kansas City. After a 4-10 year and some arm problems at Kansas City, he had a shot at the Orioles and the Cardinals. He didn't make either ball club and decided to quit.

"I had made connections with a stock market company and later worked for a steamship company. I retired in 1994," he said.

Kucks and his wife, Barbara, raised two children, have four grandchildren and have remained in the New Jersey area ever since his playing days.

"I play a lot of golf, and we have done a great deal of traveling," said Kucks. "It was a busy time when I was working in the steamship business, but now I just spend a lot of leisure time with my children and grandchildren."

Kucks is a little heavier than he was in his pitching days but still has that athletic appearance and quick smile that were trademarks of his makeup during his Yankee days.

"I didn't have a long career [six years and a 54-56 record] but I did get into four World Series and won a game that a lot of people still remember," he said. "I still get a kick going back for Old Timers days and seeing some of the guys I played with on the Yankees."

Kucks was a vital cog on that 1956 championship team and the pitcher Stengel selected over a future Hall of Famer for Game 7. Not a bad fact for a resume.

Where Have You Gone?

BOBBY COX

I t all began, really, for Bobby Cox on opening day in 1968 at Yankee Stadium.

"I was standing in the line of players as the national anthem was being played and I was on my toes. I was so nervous I couldn't put my feet on the ground," he said. "I was wondering if I could pull a hamstring just standing there on my toes.

"I looked down the line of players and I was standing near Mickey Mantle and I looked out at the centerfield monuments and the Stadium walls and I couldn't believe where I was. I had been around the game a few years by then, but this was Yankee Stadium, the House That Ruth Built, and there I was out on the field and getting ready to start a game there. It was just too much," he said.

Cox had spent seven years in the Los Angeles Dodgers organization but had never gotten out of Vero Beach in Florida, the famed longtime spring training home of the Dodgers, for a spot on the big club in Los Angeles. He had one season with the Atlanta organization as a third baseman at Richmond.

The Yankees picked up the third baseman's contract in 1968. Cox and another Yankee hopeful, Mike Ferraro, had battled all spring for the third base spot on manager Ralph Houk's rebuilding Yankees.

SEASONS WITH YANKEES: 1968-69

Best Season with Yankees: 1968

Games: 135 • **Batting Average: .229** • At-Bats: 437 • **Hits: 100** • Walks: 41 • **Strikeouts: 85** • Runs: 33 • **Home Runs: 7** • RBI: 41

The team hadn't won a pennant since 1964, and the talent remained thin.

Cox had batted .297 at Richmond the season before and was even money to win the position.

"I didn't know until I walked into the clubhouse on opening day," recalled Cox, as he sat now in his managerial office in Atlanta. "It was never announced to the press. I just looked at the lineup like I was very casual about the entire thing. I just began to shake."

Cox has managed 22 seasons in the big-leagues with a World Series title and a record 12 consecutive division titles in Atlanta. He still recalls his time as a Yankee with fondness.

"I learned so much as a member of the Yankees. I got to play with the team with the most tradition in baseball history. I got to be a teammate of Mickey's and I got to play in the most famous stadium in baseball, Yankee Stadium," he said.

Robert Joe Cox was born May 21, 1941, in Tulsa, Oklahoma. His family soon moved to California. After graduating from Selma High he attended Reedley Junior College near his home before signing with the Dodgers in 1960. He was lost in the Dodgers organization until the big break came with the Yankees.

Cox won the starting job that spring of 1968 with a sharp bat and a steady glove. He didn't have much power (nine big-league homers in two seasons) but he was a contact hitter with good bat control and a strong sense of the game.

"I think I learned more about baseball playing those two seasons with Ralph and the Yankees than I had ever learned before," he said.

Cox batted only .229 in 135 games during his first season and .219 in 85 games in his second. He was sent down to the Yankees farm club at Syracuse in 1970 and was named the player-manager of their club at Fort Lauderdale in 1971. His knees were giving him a great deal of trouble by then.

"It was really manager-player," said Cox. "I was 30 years old and I knew which direction my career was going. If I was going to stay in the game as I wanted to do, it had to be as a manager."

Cox finished fourth with Ft. Lauderdale in his first season as a manager and was promoted to the Yankees farm club at New Haven, Connecticut in the Eastern League. He finished first that year.

Four seasons at Syracuse followed in the Yankee organization from 1973 through 1976 as new Yankee owner George Steinbrenner took over control of the team. Steinbrenner started his managerial dance with holdover Ralph Houk in 1973, then moved on to Bill Virdon and finally Billy Martin late in 1975. Martin won the first Yankee pennant in a dozen years with the 1976 team, swept by the Cincinnati Reds in that year's World Series.

"I always thought I had a chance of managing the Yankees, but mostly I wanted to manage in the big-leagues," said Cox.

"I wanted to see if I could do it and be good at it, and I wanted to see if I would enjoy it. That's just the way it worked out."

With a strong foundation in the Los Angeles organization as a player and then in the Yankees organization as a player and a manager, Cox was ready when the opportunity in Atlanta presented itself in 1978.

Cox had been the Yankees first base coach in 1977 under Billy Martin as Steinbrenner kept several managers-in-waiting around the team as insurance against another Billy Martin breakdown, as was Martin's history.

A World Series win kept Martin going into the 1978 season. Cox would accept a position as a manager of the downtrodden Atlanta Braves that year.

"It was just so exciting, so satisfying for me to get the opportunity," said Cox.

"I was familiar with the Atlanta organization and I knew they were willing to spend money under the new free agent rules to get better. I went there as the manager with a lot of enthusiasm and a lot of expectations for success."

The former struggling third baseman and minor league manager now had an organization as well as an owner in Ted Turner that was willing to do what it took to make the Braves a contender.

Cox spent four seasons in Atlanta without much improvement before moving on to rebuild another down franchise in Toronto. The Blue Jays got within a game of winning the pennant in the tough American League Championship Series against Kansas City in 1985.

Cox then moved back to Atlanta as the team's general manager after that season and concentrated on improving the farm system, a key to success he had learned and witnessed with the Yankees in his years with that organization.

He remained at the desk job through June of 1990 when he went back on the field as Atlanta manager. He gave up the front office duties at the end of that season and concentrated on managing when the Braves acquired skilled GM John Schuerholz to run operations off the field.

Cox now holds the mark for most postseason wins by any manager in history and has made it to the top dozen in career regular-season victories.

While Cox's Atlanta teams have been in baseball's upper echelon for more than a dozen years, he has had only one World Series title in that time, a 1995 championship against Cleveland.

"It takes an awful lot of hard work to stay on top as we have all these years," said Cox. "Sometimes the World Series depends on the health of your team or a couple of good breaks. Maybe we haven't had the breaks."

One break Cox did get was moving to the Yankees from his time with Los Angeles and that single season as an Atlanta organization player.

"When I look back and think of my days with the Yankees, I still get pretty emotional about it. I just shake even now when I think of lining up at the Yankee Stadium and standing on my toes," he said.

Where Have You Gone?

HORACE CLARKE

There are some 16,000 baseball players who wore big-league uniforms, yet only a fraction of them ever became famous.

Eddie Gaedel, who walked for the Browns in his one appearance in a major league game, became famous for his height—three foot seven as he stood in uniform No. 1/8 for St. Louis in 1951.

Walter Alston, who struck out in his one major league at-bat for the Cardinals, was known for a later Hall of Fame managerial career with the Dodgers.

Horace Clarke became famous because he was an average big-leaguer on below-average Yankee teams for more than a decade.

Ernest Hemingway personified what became known as The Lost Generation, the World War I expatriates who settled in Paris in the 1920s. Clarke was the focal point of Yankee teams that were lost between the glory of the 1950s and early 1960s and the redemption offered by new owner George Steinbrenner in the 1970s.

The Yankees did not win a pennant during Clarke's time with the team. They actually finished 10th in 1966, finished ninth in 1967, finished sixth and fifth and snuck in for one second-place finish in 1970, only 15 games behind Baltimore.

These were dreadful seasons in declining Yankee Stadium as the crosstown New York Mets won a World Series in 1969, stayed com-

SEASONS WITH YANKEES: 1965-74

Best Season with Yankees: 1969

Games: 156 • Batting Average: .285 • At-Bats: 641 (1st in AL) • Hits: 183 (2nd in AL) • Walks: 53 • Strikeouts: 41 • Runs: 82 • Home Runs: 4 • RBI: 48 • Stolen Bases: 33 (7th in AL)

petitive almost every year, won another pennant in 1973 and electrified the city with their vibrant play.

Clarke got his average up to an impressive .285 in 156 games in 1969, but received little credit for being one of the most consistent hitters in the league.

"It never mattered the way I was written up in the press," said Clarke, as he rested near his old Yankee locker during an Old Timers Day event. "All I could do was my best. I had no control over what else happened on the team."

The pressures on Clarke were enormous as so many critics pointed out the Yankees were not an interesting or competitive team any more, and Clarke, a soft-spoken gentle man, may have been the cause.

Bobby Richardson had been the Yankee anchor at second base for the team during some golden years from 1955 through 1964. Richardson played in seven Yankee World Series.

After Yogi Berra became the manager in 1964 and was followed by Johnny Keane in 1965, Richardson and close pal Tony Kubek decided to retire. Kubek left the Yankees in trouble when he retired after the 1965 season. Richardson promised to play one more season.

As the Yankees searched for a shortstop and a second baseman to replace their dynamic duo, Clarke was moving up in the organization.

He played with Richardson in 1965 and 1966 and inherited the second-base job in 1967. He played in 143 games, batted .272, collected 160 hits as a switch hitter and played an adequate—only adequate—second base.

"Bobby helped me a lot before he retired," Clarke said. "But he was a different player. I couldn't play the way he had played."

Clarke's fielding abilities probably sat in the middle of the American League's second baseman the way his batting abilities sat in the middle of the league's hitters.

Everything about his game seemed average—his hitting, his fielding, his range, his speed (33 stolen bases in 1969 was impressive) and his intensity.

The more the Yankees lost—and they lost plenty in those days—the more the media and the fans concentrated on Clarke as the cause. He was not the cause. He was no different, no better or worse, than dozens of other Yankee players who came through the Stadium gates in those years.

"I always did my best. I always played as hard as I could. I never was concerned about how the fans reacted to me," he said.

While he was often an object of ridicule by the media, many of whom specialized as cheap shot artists, Clarke retained his dignity. He showed up for work every day without complaint, did his job and hoped for improvement.

Horace Meredith Clarke was born in Frederiksted, Virgin Islands on June 2, 1940. He played lots of baseball as a small child and was soon starring on many amateur baseball teams. Baseball was a passion in his home country, and his friends and neighbors cheered when he was signed by the Yankees.

"I remember the first game I played in Yankee stadium in 1965. There were more than 40,000 people in the stands. I had just come from my country where there are 30,000 people in the entire country. That was some adjustment," he said.

Speaking English with the lilt of the islands, Clarke soon became a favorite of his teammates who rallied around him as the press scorned him. In that depressing 10th-place 1966 season when Houk came back to manage after Johnny Keane was fired, Clarke performed well. He batted .266 and proved a successful leadoff man with 27 walks and only 24 strikeouts.

"I always concentrated on getting the bat on the ball," he said.

"I would try to hit the ball where it was pitched. I also got a lot of hits with my legs."

He stood five foot nine and weighed 170 pounds at his best playing weight. There were times when he seemed to be one of the best base runners in the league, and few pitchers found him an easy out.

He had a .256 lifetime average after spending a decade with the Yankees and 42 games with San Diego in 1974 at the end of his career.

Clarke returned home to the Virgin Islands, opened up a baseball school for youngsters and encouraged many of his students that they could find fame and fortune in big-league baseball.

"I had a nice career in the big-leagues," he said. "I didn't play on any World Series teams but I played for the Yankees for a long time. There are some wonderful memories about that, especially playing with Mickey [Mantle], Whitey [Ford], Elston [Howard] and the rest."

Horace Clarke took a public beating, clearly undeserved in his Yankee time, mostly because he wasn't Bobby Richardson. Not many second basemen are.

He played hard, he was never contentious, and he never blamed anyone else for the down years. Horace Clarke deserved better.

Maybe one of the kids he is working with in the Virgin Islands will carry Clarke's banner high when he goes on to star among those exceptional big-leaguers.

Dooley Womack

Hank Bauer (left) and Bill Skowron

Bill Werber

Sparky Lyle

Art Ditmar

Phil Linz

Bud Daley

Mike Hegan

Bobby Murcer (left) and Maury Allen

Ron Klimkowski

Willie Randolph

Joe DeMaestri

George Zeber

Bob Cerv

Rollie Sheldon

Fran Healy

Bucky Dent (left) and Mike Torrez

JAY
JOHNSTONE

There are horses for courses, the followers of the Sport of Kings like to suggest, when certain thoroughbreds can excel at one track and nap at another.

Jay Johnstone was made for the Yankees.

Nobody ever looked better in his pinstripes. Johnstone could have been the poster boy for what Yankees are supposed to look like: Six foot one, a streamlined 175 pounds, with dark eyes and dark hair and that incredible handsome face.

He was born and raised in Manchester, Connecticut, but he made his baseball name in California with the Angels, played for Oakland and spent some time with the White Sox and the Phillies before making his mark in New York.

The Phillies traded Johnstone to the Yankees on June 14, 1978 in a deal for relief pitcher Rawly Eastwick.

"That was really exciting for me," Johnstone recalled. "I had been in the playoffs with the Phillies in the two previous seasons. We hadn't won, and I thought the Yankees would give me a chance to be with a winner."

Relief pitcher Sparky Lyle had labeled the team "The Bronx Zoo" and Johnstone fit in perfectly. This was a team led by manager

NEW YORK YANKEES

JAY JOHNSTONE OUTFIELD

SEASONS WITH YANKEES: 1978-79

Best Season with Yankees: 1978

Games: 36 (as a Yankee) • **Batting Average: .262** • At-Bats: 65 •
Hits: 17 • Runs: 6 • **Home Runs: 1** • RBI: 6

Billy Martin and included some of the highest profile players in the game in Reggie Jackson, Thurman Munson, Lou Piniella, Goose Gossage, Graig Nettles and Catfish Hunter.

"I enjoyed the excitement of being around these guys. The press made a big deal out of everything with [George] Steinbrenner and Billy, and I enjoyed reading the papers each day about these adventures and talking it all over with the guys in the clubhouse and in the hangout places at night," he said.

The 1978 season really exploded in late July when Martin, walking through the O'Hare airport in Chicago, told a couple of New York sportswriters his opinion of outfielder Reggie Jackson and owner George Steinbrenner.

"One's a born liar," he said of Jackson "and the other's convicted." Steinbrenner had pleaded no contest to a charge of illegal campaign contributions to the Nixon reelection fund during the Watergate era.

Johnstone had only played a month and a half for Billy Martin when the Yankee manager resigned in Kansas City in light of his combative comments. Bob Lemon, a Hall of Fame pitcher with the Cleveland Indians and a calm personality, was the new field leader.

"When I first got to the Yankees there was a fuss and a furor almost every day around Martin and Reggie and the rest. Now, with Lemon, it was just about winning. Reggie got hot and we really started to win," Johnstone said.

The Yankees began chewing away at the huge Boston lead that had grown to 14 games. Being used as a platoon player and occasional defensive outfielder, Johnstone contributed to the Yankee surge.

He batted .262 in 32 games, shored up the Yankee outfield defense and added a smiling presence on the bench.

"Jay was a cheerleader type who was very enthusiastic on the bench," said teammate Lou Piniella. "He was a great guy around the club."

At the age of 32 that season, Johnstone knew his best days were behind him. He also knew his first shot at a World Series after 12 years in the big-leagues could be in front of him.

"I accepted my role with that team," he said.

"When I was a younger player I used to howl and get very unhappy when I didn't play. On the Yankees, with all that talent, I knew I just had to stay ready when they called on me."

John William Johnstone was born on November 20, 1945. He was a schoolboy star and was signed by the expansion California Angels when he graduated from high school in 1963.

By 1965, at the age of 20, he made the Angels and fit in perfectly. The Angels were a wild bunch of California players, including Cy Young winner Dean Chance, the running mate of playboy ballplayer Bo Belinsky, hip shortstop Jim Fregosi and iconoclast Vic Power under the direction of laissez faire skipper Bill Rigney.

"That was just a bunch of fun guys on that team," said Johnstone. "They understood that you had to have a good time if you were playing this crazy game."

He had a couple of decent seasons with the Angels and then was traded to the White Sox. He moved on to Oakland and then to Philadelphia where he had four sparkling seasons and made it to the NLCS in 1976 and 1977.

The Yankees needed a pinch hitter and a backup outfielder in 1978 and acquired Johnstone in a deal with the Phillies for reliever Rawley Eastwick.

"That was pretty exciting for me to get to the Yankees at that stage of my career. I think every big-league ball player dreams of a shot with the Yankees. All that history, all that attention and playing in Yankee Stadium. That's impressive stuff," he said.

Johnstone was sent to San Diego and then to the Dodgers, Cubs, and back to the Dodgers for his final season in 1985. He was 39 years old.

Johnstone spent 20 years in the big-leagues, batted .267, played on two Series winners, including 1981 with the Dodgers against some of his old Yankee pals, and left with a smile on his face.

He was back on the golf course near his home in Pasadena, California after he retired and worked frequently for local radio and television stations.

"It was a great run," he said. "I got 20 years on my big-league pension so I don't have to work the rest of my life. That's not a bad goal to reach."

FRAN HEALY

Billy Martin stood in the center of the visiting team clubhouse before a scheduled game that summer night in 1977 against the Detroit Tigers.

The Yankee players surrounded the manager as he ranted and raved about the conduct of his team, backup catcher Fran Healy remembered.

"No more carrying on in here," Martin screamed. "No more horsing around on the bench. No more hot foots. No more laughing during the game. We gotta get serious."

The Yankees moved soberly to the field where a steady rain was falling. As Martin climbed the top step of the dugout he saw the umpires wave their arms. The game was called off.

"OK," shouted Martin, "let's go drink."

Healy was sitting in the New York Mets pressroom at Shea Stadium in Queens, New York, as he laughed at his fondest Yankee memory of that memorable World Championship season.

"Then the day after Reggie [Jackson] hit those three World Series homers against the Dodgers, I met him early in the morning to film a motivational project. We had made up to do that a month earlier after our final game. He had been on all the television shows

NEW YORK YANKEES

FRAN **HEALY** CATCHER

SEASONS WITH YANKEES: 1976-78

Best Season with Yankees: 1976

Games: 46 (as a Yankee) • **Batting Average: .267** • At-Bats: 120 • **Hits: 32** • Runs: 10 • **Home Runs: 0** • RBI: 9

because of the homers, but I still grabbed him, got him into a car and went to our studio," Healy said.

Healy was the closest Yankee to Jackson and probably the only teammate who could summon the famed Mr. October from his television rounds.

The event also changed Healy's life.

"I was out of the lineup with an injury that season and I went to the broadcast booth with Phil Rizzuto. I did the game and George [Steinbrenner] heard it and liked me. The next year I became a broadcaster and I have been doing it ever since," he said.

Healy was obtained by the Yankees in May of 1976 for pitcher Larry Gura, Billy Martin's least favorite Yankee.

"Billy started me in a game and put Thurman [Munson] in the outfield. I don't know if that was his plan, to get both of us in the lineup with me behind the plate, but a couple of fly balls hit Thurman on the head and that was it. Thurman was a great athlete, but he couldn't play the outfield," Healy said.

Francis Xavier Healy was born in Holyoke, Massachusetts, on September 6, 1946. An uncle, Francis Xavier Paul Healy, had played for the New York Giants and the 1934 world champion St. Louis Cardinals, the famous Gashouse Gang team led by manager Frankie Frisch and stars Dizzy and Paul Dean, Leo Durocher, Pepper Martin and Joe Medwick.

"There was a lot of baseball talk around my family. I heard all those Gashouse Gang stories from my uncle," Healy said.

As an 18-year-old, he signed with the Cleveland Indians but continued in school at Holyoke College and later American International University.

"I went to spring training with the Indians and drove to the ball park one day with Rocky Colavito and Don McMahon. That was a thrill. We had to be there early because Marvin Miller was coming in to talk about the union," Healy said.

His time in the Cleveland organization was a difficult experience for Healy. The Indians wanted him to serve out his military obligation so he could play full time for them. Instead he attended college and only played a few minor league games.

"[Cleveland GM] Sid Thrift said I could make the big-leagues if I stopped treating the Indians as if they were a summer league team," Healy said.

After playing only in July and August while school was out, Cleveland gave up on Healy and sent him to the Kansas City Royals. He played a few games and then entered military service.

He was traded to San Francisco for the 1971 season, stayed there in 1972 and was traded back to Kansas City where he remained for the next three years. He had his best season in 1974 where he hit .252 in 134 games with nine homers. Healy would hit only 11 additional homers in his nine-year career.

"Some guys can hit home runs and some guys can't. I had a line-drive swing, and I couldn't lift the ball in the air. Hank Aaron started with a cross-handed swing when he broke in and couldn't lift the ball. I guess he changed and I didn't," Healy said.

"I was happy when I came to the Yankees. I knew this was a chance to be on a winner. We won in 1976 and lost the Series to Cincinnati but won it all in 1977. I got my World Series ring, and my uncle has his from the Cardinals. I got another in 1986 as a broadcaster with the Mets," he said.

Healy went to spring training with the Yankees in 1978, had one at-bat when the season started and then got a call from Steinbrenner.

"Would you like to go to the booth?" the Boss asked.

"Absolutely," said Healy.

He joined the Yankee broadcast crew on radio, soon moved to cable television where he did both Mets and Yankee games and has spent the last 20 years as a Mets television broadcaster.

"I played on the western champion Giants in 1971 and Yankee winners in 1976 and 1977. I have been in the game for almost 40 years now. I think that is pretty good," he said.

Healy batted .250 with only 20 homers in his career but may have saved the Yankees in 1977 as a player and 1978 as a broadcaster in his closeness to Reggie Jackson.

"We were good friends. He liked to talk, and I was willing to listen. He is a bright guy, and with my degree I am supposed to be a closet intellectual," said Healy. "I enjoyed being with him."

Every time Jackson seemed near a fatal explosion as a Yankee, Healy served as a moderating force. He contributed significantly to Jackson's New York success—four division titles in five seasons, three American league pennants and one World Series championship.

Healy and his wife, Gloria, have two daughters, Debbie and Kara, and still make their home in Holyoke.

"My Yankee time was so long ago I can hardly remember it now," said Healy. "What I do remember always seems to be positive."

FRANK
TEPEDINO

On September 11, 2001 Frank Tepedino, a New York City Fire Department lieutenant and former New York Yankee outfielder for four of his eight big-league seasons, sat at the kitchen table of his Baldwin, Long Island, New York home.

He was off that day, and he and his son, Frank Jr., also a NYC firefighter, drank coffee, kidded about the laughs they had on recent rounds and planned some family weekend activities.

The television set was on low as background noise.

"I just heard someone say on the news that a plane had gone into the World Trade Center," Tepedino recalled as he visited Yankee Stadium for an Old Timers weekend. "I immediately thought that it was probably a pilot who had a heart attack. I remember reading the story about a plane that went into the Empire State Building in 1946 in a big fog. I thought it was something like that."

This day was different, a crystal clear late summer morning in New York City, thousands of people inside the building at 8:48 a.m. and thousands more walking to work around the area.

"Then came the second crash into the other tower," said Tepedino. "I knew this wasn't an accident. I knew this was serious and I had to be there."

SEASONS WITH YANKEES: 1967-71; 1972

Best Season with Yankees: 1970

Games: 16 • **Batting Average:** .316 • At-Bats: 19 • **Hits:** 6 • Runs: 2 • **Home Runs:** 0 • RBI: 2

The former Yankee and his son ran for the car and raced down the Long Island Expressway into lower Manhattan. They drove to their station house, Patrol 2 on West Third Street.

The world knew by then of the dastardly terrorist attack on the New York City business complex, thousands trapped inside the burning buildings, thousands more stumbling through the flames, the smoke and the confusion.

The two towers fell before the 53-year-old Tepedino, a New York City firefighter for 22 years after his baseball career ended, arrived on the scene.

There were 343 firefighters lost, blood brothers for Tepedino and all other firefighters, in the shattered ruins of the World Trade Center.

"I worked 24 hours without a break, searching for friends, pulling rubble off bodies, breathing that dust, hoping we could rescue some of our guys," he said.

It wasn't to be.

Tepedino went home, finally, for a few hours' rest. He returned to the World Trade Center site the next day after reporting in to his station near Thompson Street and Sullivan Place, within sight of the once-imposing towers.

"There was a kid who had worked with me. His name was Keith Roma. He was 26, very handsome and bright. He had a terrific future with the NYFD. He was missing," Tepedino remembered.

A block or two from the scene of the disaster he saw a crushed fire truck. It was filled with dirt and dust. No one was near the truck.

"I walked over and climbed up the front. I saw a Yankee baseball cap sitting on the front seat. It was dusty but intact. Right under the *NY* logo I could read the name scribbled in pen. Keith Roma. I knew," he said.

Tepedino was in Yankee Stadium the following summer with many of his teammates from the Yankees of 1967 through 1971. Bobby Murcer was the star of some of those teams. He and Tepedino had remained close.

"Frank called me and told me about his friend. He told me about the baseball cap. I got a few caps and had some of the guys, Derek Jeter, Jason Giambi, Bernie Williams and even Joe Torre sign them for the Roma family," said Murcer.

"Keith cared only about two things—the job and the Yankees. These Yankee caps meant so much to his family," Tepedino said.

Frank Ronald Tepedino was born in Brooklyn on November 23, 1947. He was a high school baseball All-Star at Brooklyn's Lafayette High and was signed by the Yankees as soon as he graduated high school.

He made it to the Yankees in 1967 as a 19 year old, played nine games on a Yankee team with Mickey Mantle in centerfield, came back for 13 games in 1969 and 16 more in 1970 before being traded to Milwaukee.

Tepedino was returned to the Yankees in 1972 and was moved to Atlanta for the final three years of his career in 1973, 1974 and 1975.

In eight big-league seasons the left-handed-hitting outfielder batted .241 with six big-league home runs.

"I never made any money in baseball, but I loved the game. I thought I might try and stay in it as a coach or manager, but nothing opened up. I had always been interested in the NYFD. I took the test and won my appointment in 1980," he said.

While he enjoyed every minute of his NYFD work—until 9/11/01—he also loved to entertain his pals with baseball stories.

"They all know I'm kind of an historic baseball figure. I'm the only guy who was on the field for Mickey Mantle's 500th career homer in 1967 and Hank Aaron's record-breaking 715th homer in 1974," he said.

The Yankees were a family tradition for Tepedino, but the firefighter part of his professional career took over after he joined the department. Two of his sons and a brother are also on the job in NYC.

"We lost so many guys, close pals to all of us, on 9/11," said Tepedino. "No one on the job that day can ever forget where he was, what he did, how he reacted when he heard the news."

In the clubhouse of the New York Yankees in 2002, Tepedino looked trim and strong with a rugged face and gray hair as he chatted with a lot of old baseball friends.

"Playing for the Yankees was a lifetime experience. I'll never forget a moment of it," he said. "I won't ever forget 9/11. I hope nobody in this country does."

Where Have You Gone?

BOBBY MURCER

Bobby Murcer, a Yankee outfielder in 13 of his 17 big-league seasons, was called "Lemon" for his soft, round, cherubic face by kidding teammates.

He hit 252 home runs in his career and was just about the only star worth watching in his first tour of duty with the downtrodden Yankees from 1965 through 1974.

Murcer had been a teammate, friend and counsel for Thurman Munson ever since the tense, insecure, talented catcher had joined the Yankees in 1969. His bulky body, five foot 11 and about 190 pounds, had earned Munson the nicknames "Squatty Body," a tag put on him by pitcher Fritz Peterson, and "Tugboat," as Murcer called him.

Murcer used the nickname on September 6, 1979, as he delivered the eulogy for his friend at the Canton Memorial Civic Center before 500 friends and family inside and another thousand fans of the catcher outside the building.

Munson had been killed in a plane crash as he piloted his own Cessna into Canton-Akron Airport at 3:02 P.M. on August 2, 1979, when the plane crashed a thousand feet shy of runway 19. The Yankee captain was 32 years old.

NEW YORK YANKEES

BOBBY
MURCER OUTFIELD

SEASONS WITH YANKEES: 1965-74; 1979-83

Best Season for Yankees: 1972 (All-Star; Gold Glove; fifth in MVP voting)

Games: 153 (fourth in AL) • **Batting Average:** .292 (10th in AL) • At-Bats: 585 (fifth in AL) • **Hits:** 171 (third in AL) • Runs: 102 (first in AL) • Doubles: 30 (third in AL) • **Triples: 7 (fourth in AL)** • Home Runs: 33 (second in AL) • **RBI: 96 (third in AL)** • BB: 63 • **Strikeouts: 67** • Slugging Percentage: .537 (third in AL) • **Total Bases: 314 (first in AL)**

Murcer stood at the rostrum of the Civic Center that day, looked at the catcher's widow, Diane, made eye contact with all of his teammates and owner George Steinbrenner and manager Billy Martin in the front row and began talking of his pal.

"He lived, he led, he loved. Whatever he was to each of us—catcher, captain, competitor, husband, father, friend—he should be remembered as a man who valued and followed the basic principles of life...

"As Lou Gehrig led the Yankees as the captain of the '30s, our Thurman Munson captained the Yankees of the '70s. Someone someday shall earn that right to lead this team again, for that is how Thurm—Tugboat, as I called him, would want it. He wore No. 15 on the field, but in living, loving and legend, history will record Thurman as Number One."

"It's so many years now," said Murcer, as he sat on the bench at Yankee Stadium in 2003 before broadcasting a Yankee game. "I still get choked up when I think about it. I never felt that kind of emotion."

George Steinbrenner kept Munson's memory alive by keeping his Stadium locker permanently emptied of all equipment except the metal identification plate with 15 on it.

"I walk by the locker and say 'Hi' to Thurm. It is especially tough around that August 2 date when the Yankees show clips of his career on the big scoreboard screen," Murcer said.

If Thurman Munson was Murcer's best baseball friend, the New York Yankees were the best part of his baseball life.

"I just forget about those years with the Giants and Cubs," he said.

If ever a left-handed hitter was made for the Stadium, it was Bobby Murcer. He hit as many as 33 homers for the Yankees in 1972. He fell to 10 in 1974 when the Yankees spent the season at Shea Stadium in Queens while Yankee Stadium was being remodeled.

"That was a horror," he recalled. "The wind was against me all the time, the walls were more distant and the site lines were more difficult."

He specialized in hitting balls about 325 feet in a stadium where the fence was 338 feet away.

"Warning Track Bobby," became his needling nickname.

Bobby Ray Murcer was born May 20, 1946 in Oklahoma City, Oklahoma. After a sparkling high school career, the Yankees signed Murcer and brought him to the Stadium for the first time in 1965. He was 19 years old.

Hardly any Yankee since Mickey Mantle's arrival in 1951 (with Joe DiMaggio as team icon) underwent the pressure of the media that Murcer was subjected to.

He was from Oklahoma, as Mantle was, he was very young as Mantle was when he joined the Yankees, he was a good-looking slugger, and he was destined to replace the aging Mantle.

"I played shortstop when I broke in, but Johnny Keane moved me quickly to the outfield. He thought I would hurt too many people behind first base with my throws," Murcer said.

Mantle had also started as a shortstop who threw wildly. The connections became the focus of media attention. Mantle, unlike DiMaggio in his time, was helpful.

"Mickey just took care of me," he said. "He told me to play my own game and not to worry about comparisons or competition."

Murcer hit only .243 and .174 in parts of two seasons before leaving for military service. He returned in 1969 after Mantle retired and batted .259 with 26 home runs. He was on his way to Yankee stardom.

Murcer was the slugging star of the Yankees for the next five seasons. On October 22, 1974, he was traded to the Giants for Bobby Bonds, father of baseball's later home run king, Barry Bonds, who hit a record 73 in 2001.

"That was just a terrible blow. I hated San Francisco. I hated the wind, and the team wasn't going anywhere," Murcer said.

He went to the Cubs where conditions weren't much better for the 1977, 1978 and part of 1979 seasons. Then he came back to the Yankees on June 26, 1979.

He lost his best pal about five weeks later.

After the Yankees flew back from Munson's funeral in Canton, they played the Baltimore Orioles at the Stadium. The catcher's spot was left open when the team took the field until substitute Jerry Narron jogged on to the field.

The Orioles led 4-0 that Friday night until Murcer hit a three-run home run off Dennis Martinez, his first Yankee Stadium homer since September 28, 1973.

Then he hit a game-winning single with two runners on base in the bottom of the ninth inning for a 5-4 Yankee victory in one of the most emotional triumphs in team history.

He played in the postseason for the Yankees for the first time in 1980 and made it to the World Series against the Dodgers in 1981, some 16 years after he first put on pinstripes.

"That was pretty satisfying after that long wait," he said.

He played with the team as a pinch hitter in 1982 and 1983 before moving upstairs to the broadcast booth.

He and his wife, Kay, still make their home in Oklahoma City where Bobby spends the winters in business pursuits, including operating a wholesale jewelry business and dealing in cattle investing. They have two children and became grandparents for the first time in 2003.

"I can remember the first day I walked on the field here," Murcer said, as he looked out over the Stadium grass. "I was so nervous I could hardly breathe. I still get chills when I walk on the field. This is Yankee Stadium. There is no place in the game like it."

Where Have You Gone?

CLETE
BOYER

O n December 17, 1985, more than a dozen former New York
Yankee ballplayers gathered at the St. Mary's Roman Catholic
Church in Fargo, North Dakota, for an evening visitation before the
following day's funeral of Roger Maris.

The Yankee slugger and two-time MVP, who had set a new
single-season home run record of 61 in 1961 in passing the Babe
Ruth mark of 60 set in 1927, had died a few days earlier after a long
battle with cancer.

Now the players had flown from all over to honor their teammate and be with the Maris family. Mickey Mantle and Whitey Ford
had flown up from a golf tournament in Florida. They were each
wearing summer clothes as they walked off the plane at the small
airport.

"How cold is it?" asked Mantle, as he scurried through the airport wearing a thin, black leather jacket over his sport clothes, a cowboy shirt open at the collar and rusty cowboy boots.

Told by a reporter greeting him that was it 17 degrees below
zero, Mantle howled a long obscenity. "You got a drink in your van?"
he asked Don Gooselaw, a Maris family friend assigned to pick up the
two Hall of Famers.

SEASONS WITH YANKEES: 1959-66

Best Season with Yankees: 1962

Games: 158 • **Batting Average: .272** • At-Bats: 566 • **Hits: 154** •
Runs: 85 • **Doubles: 24** • Home Runs: 18 • **RBI: 68**

There were several hundred people at the church that night with one row saved for the Maris teammates including Mantle, Ford, Bill Skowron, John Blanchard, Ryne Duren, Bobby Richardson, Tony Kubek and Clete Boyer.

Bishop James S. Sullivan conducted the services, intoned some words to God, offered up prayers for Maris and called on friends to reminisce about the fallen Yankee warrior.

Many local people and lifelong friends spoke of Maris. Bishop Sullivan asked if anyone else would talk of Maris as he looked clearly at the row of former ballplayers. None of them moved.

Finally, Boyer, a teammate of Maris on the Yankees for seven seasons from 1960 to 1966, rose quietly from his seat. He walked forward to the rostrum.

"My name is Clete Boyer. I was a teammate of Roger's," he began.

He talked warmly, eloquently for some minutes about his friend, presenting an intimate portrait of a complex man. He made the audience of friends and family laugh as he described details of dinners with Roger as he put away huge quantities of food. Then he sat down.

"That was the most nervous I had ever been in my life," Boyer said later. "I knew one of us had to talk."

That evening, Boyer came through in another clutch situation for the Yankees—albeit at the funeral of a friend—saving the players from embarrassment at not being willing to publicly applaud their teammate.

Cletis LeRoy Boyer, one of seven Boyer boys (the perfect-planning Boyers also had seven girls) was born February 8, 1937, in the rural farming community of Cassville, Missouri. He and older brother, Ken Boyer, broke into the big-leagues in the same season of 1955, Ken as a third baseman with the Cardinals and Clete as a shortstop for the Kansas City Athletics.

Ken established himself as a star with a .306 batting average in his second season, while Clete had to struggle for success with a weak bat.

Clete Boyer batted .242 in 16 big-league seasons with the A's, the Yankees and the Atlanta Braves. He hit 26 home runs for Atlanta in his first season there in 1967.

It was with his glove that he made his big-league mark. He was one of the premier third basemen in the game during his time with

raging arguments from fans and sportswriters alike about the relative skills of Hall of Famer Brooks Robinson and Boyer at third base.

His Yankee manager, Ralph Houk, always credited Boyer as well as Mantle and Maris, the M and M Boys, for the incredible 1961 season.

"Defense wins baseball games," Houk said. "That's why Clete was so important to us."

"I always took as much pride with my glove as most guys take with their bats," Boyer said. "I worked hard to become as good as I could."

Some of his fielding plays at third were of the spectacular kind as he would often dive across the foul line at third, back hand a ball, turn rapidly, and from awkward positions rifle the baseball to first base for an out.

"My arm was always strong," he said.

"That was just natural for me. I could cover more ground and play deeper than other third basemen because of my strong arm."

He became the regular Yankee third baseman under Casey Stengel in 1960. He also suffered his worst baseball embarrassment that year. Stengel sent up a pinch hitter for Boyer in the second inning of the first Series game.

"That hurt, but it was Casey's way," said Boyer.

He played on five straight Series teams from 1960 to 1964 with championships in 1961 and 1962. Overall he batted .233 in 27 Series games, but observers raved about his defense.

"I broke in as a shortstop and always played third base like a shortstop. I covered as much ground as I could and took away a lot of hits by being quick," he said.

Playing with Mantle and Maris, Boyer always tried to compete with the sluggers in the long ball category. He did well against them in batting practice but often hit long fly ball outs to centerfield when the games started.

"I think I could have some big numbers if I had played at a small stadium like the one in Atlanta instead of Yankee Stadium," he said.

He served as a Yankee coach and minor league instructor for the Yankees for many years after his retirement. He also opened up a hamburger store in Cooperstown, New York, home of Baseball's Hall of Fame, where he could be found often in summer months signing autographs for customers while turning over hamburgers on a grill.

He and his wife, Terry, have six children and a dozen grandchildren. They make their home in Bellair Beach, Florida.

"I still get a thrill when I get back to Yankee Stadium," he said. "I cried the first time I went out to Monument Park and saw those monuments and plaques for Babe Ruth and Lou Gehrig. I still cry when I walk out there."

STEVE
BALBONI

He hit some of the longest, highest, hardest home runs seen in the American League since Babe Ruth was hitting moon shots into the third deck of old Yankee Stadium.

Steve Balboni looked a bit like the Babe, standing six foot three and weighing a stocky 225 pounds. He spent two tours with the Yankees—from 1981 to 1983, before Don Mattingly claimed first base for a decade, and again in 1989 and 1990 as Mattingly's career was winding down.

Balboni joined the Yankees when they were still a World Series team in 1981—the one loss George Steinbrenner apologized publicly for—and was with them in their next two declining years.

Bob Watson, John Mayberry and even Ken Griffey Sr. filled the first-base role while the Yankees waited for the strong right-handed hitter to show some consistency. In a year or so it didn't much matter as Mattingly came along to claim the position and proved to be one of the most talented hitters in Yankee history.

"I grew up in Massachusetts and I was a Red Sox fan of course," said Balboni from his home in Berkeley Heights, New Jersey. "But when I signed with the Yankees and put that uniform on I really fell in love with the team, the history and the tradition."

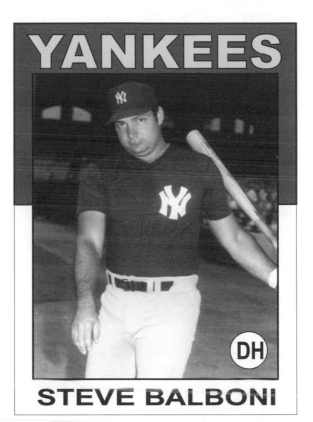

YANKEES

STEVE BALBONI

SEASONS WITH YANKEES: 1981-83;
1989-90

Best Season with Yankees: 1989

Games: 110 • **Batting Average:** .237 • At-Bats: 300 • **Hits:** 71 •
Runs: 33 • **Home Runs:** 17 • RBI: 59

Using a heavy bat, 36 inches and 38 ounces, Balboni's blasts earned him the nickname "Bye-Bye," and fans would scream as he lofted one of his high drives to the deepest part of left or left center field in the spacious Stadium.

He only hit seven homers in his early tour with the Yankees but slugged 17 in each of his final two seasons, some of them racing for the back streets of the Bronx before crashing into an upper deck location.

"I always swung hard. That's why I guess I didn't hit for average," he said.

Balboni compiled a .228 lifetime average in 10 big-league seasons but peaked at the right time. He was traded to Kansas City in 1983 and had his finest year with the world champion Royals in 1985 when he batted .243, hit 36 homers and knocked in 88 runs for the champions. He also led the league in strikeouts with 166, indicating that he was not giving in to any pitcher when he stood strong at home plate.

"That 1985 season was just such a wonderful year," he said. "It really was an exceptional team and we have stayed very close through the years. I see a lot of the Kansas City guys as I travel around."

Kansas City was down to Toronto two games in the playoffs but rallied to win. They lost the first two games at home to St. Louis in the World Series and fell back three games to one. The Royals, under manager Dick Howser, became the first Series team to win after losing the first two at home and only the sixth team ever to rally from a 3-1 deficit for a World Series crown.

Balboni was not only a vital cog in the success of the team during the regular season with his sparkling year, but also in the postseason. After a weak American League Championship Series, he shined in the October classic with a .320 mark in seven games.

"We had a terrific team with great pitching. That was the year [Bret] Saberhagen was the best in the game, Charlie Leibrandt had a great season and [Dan] Quisenberry was unhittable out of the bullpen," Balboni said.

George Brett had one of his routine .335 seasons with 30 homers and 112 runs batted in to anchor the offense.

Stephen Charles Balboni was born January 16, 1957, in Brockton, Massachusetts, a town made famous by legendary heavyweight champion Rocky Marciano.

He was a high school baseball All-Star and earned a scholarship to Eckerd College in St. Petersburg, Florida near the spring training homes of the New York Mets and the St. Louis Cardinals.

"They often worked out on our field before the spring training camps opened, so I got to know a lot of the major league players," Balboni said.

He signed with the Yankees after his third year at Eckerd and joined the team for the first time late in 1981 under recycled manager Bob Lemon, the hero-savior of the famous 1978 comeback season.

It was a strike season with two separate halves and the Yankees, knowing they were in the playoffs for winning the first half, played lazily in the second half. It cost Gene Michael his managerial job. Lemon was brought in but couldn't get the Yankees motivated enough for a World Series win. Los Angeles defeated the Yankees four games to two after losing the first two games in the Stadium.

Owner Steinbrenner felt so ashamed at his team's collapse he issued a public apology after the final game, a universal source of snickering for all media types and most fans.

Balboni moved on to Kansas City, stayed with the team into 1988, was traded to Seattle and came back to the Yankees for his final two seasons.

He retired at the age of 33 after the 1990 season. He batted only .192 with an impressive 17 homers but had back and knee troubles that forced him to the sidelines.

"I knew I wanted to stay in the game but nothing opened up," he said. "I stayed home with my family, just relaxed and considered what I would do next."

Balboni and his wife, Eve, have three sons, Daniel, now 18, Matthew, 15, and Michael, 13.

"After staying home a few years I began writing letters to ball clubs asking for a spot in their organization. Five years ago the Royals said they had a position in their rookie league team as a hitting instructor. The season was only three months long so I took it to try it out," he said. "It turned out that I really liked helping kids."

Balboni worked for the Royals, the Montreal Expos and then the St. Louis Cardinals. In 2002 he was hired as the hitting instructor for the Double A Tennessee Smokies in Knoxville. He returned to that position in 2003.

"I don't teach the kids my hitting style. I probably swung too hard. I just get them to be comfortable in their own style. I learned a lot about hitting watching other hitters throughout my career, especially a classic hitter like George Brett," he said.

Balboni said he had several young players on the Smokies with a chance at the big-leagues. One prospect, Yadier Molina, 20 years old, is considered a sure-fire big-leaguer.

"Sometimes a kid you work with goes up to the big-leagues and it helps your chances of getting there. I'm still young [at age 46] and I have hope that I can get a big-league job before too long. All you can do is wait for the call," he said.

Steve "Bye Bye" Balboni hit some shots the Babe would have been proud of in his time. Now, he might teach some other youngster how to aim for the third deck at Yankee Stadium.

Where Have You Gone?

CLIFF
JOHNSON

After 10 seasons in the Houston organization, Cliff Johnson joined the Yankees for 56 games in 1977, a full season with 76 games played in the fabled 1978 Yankee year and 26 more Yankee games in 1979 before moving on to Cleveland.

"I played 15 seasons in the big-leagues with seven teams, but all anybody asks about is the Yankees. That was the greatest soap opera ever. 'Let's see the World Series ring.' That's what they all say," Johnson said.

On October 2, 1978, the Yankees played the Boston Red Sox at Fenway Park in the second American League playoff game. Cleveland had defeated the Red Sox in the 1948 game. Now Bucky Dent would gain baseball immortality with a seventh-inning three-run homer off Mike Torrez, leading to a 5-4 Yankee win for the AL East title.

"I can't remember a thing about the game, not even Bucky's homer. I was too damn nervous. Oh no, not about the game, about the birth of my first child, Dana Monet Johnson," the former catcher-first baseman-designated hitter-outfielder said.

"My wife, Pamela, was giving birth to our daughter, and I was a pile of nerves. As the game went on I was going back and forth to the

NEW YORK YANKEES

CLIFF
JOHNSON · CATCHER

SEASONS WITH YANKEES: 1977-79

Best Season with Yankees: 1977

Games: 56 (as a Yankee) • **Batting Average: .296** • At-Bats: 142
• **Hits: 42** • Runs: 24 • **Home Runs: 12** • RBI: 31

pay phone and calling the hospital to speak with relatives who were there. 'Did she give birth yet?' I don't think I saw Bucky's homer. I think I was on the phone," he said.

Cliff Johnson was a big bear of a man—six foot four, a bruising 220 pounds with large hands and large feet. He was a right-handed hitter with good power and slugged 196 home runs in 15 big-league seasons.

Johnson was a tough catcher, hard to move from his spot on a tag play at the plate, a sure-handed first baseman and an outfielder with surprising speed.

He had a .258 lifetime average with a career high of .304 in 1984 with Toronto. Mostly, he was an intimidating hitter with a ferocious cut.

"I never got cheated," he said.

As big and strong as he was, Johnson was a smiling, friendly presence around the Yankees with an easy acceptance of his role as backup catcher to captain Thurman Munson.

"I played with a lot of teams and had a lot of fun in the game, but the Yankee years were so special. I lived in Houston when I was playing there, and nobody knew me, but when I went back home to San Antonio after playing with the Yankees everybody knew me," he said.

Clifford Johnson Jr., nicknamed Heathcliff after a television character, was born July 22, 1947, near the Alamo in San Antonio, Texas.

He now lives on a 117-acre ranch nearby in the town of Schertz where he raises cattle and quarterhorses. He is married to his second wife, Christine, a lieutenant colonel nurse-practitioner in the U. S. Army.

"I don't have as many head of cattle as I used to have," he said. "The bottom really fell out of the cattle market a few years back. We do well with the quarterhorses and race a lot of them in the area. Right now I am involved in getting some capital together for a real estate project near our ranch. Everybody always seems to do well in real estate."

He recently played golf in a San Antonio charity tournament for an Alzheimer's fundraiser with Hall of Famer Harmon Killebrew.

"Everybody was coming up for autographs. I was wearing a Yankee cap. It just sets you apart. I cherish those days," Johnson said.

He spent six seasons with Houston before being traded to the Yankees for the 1977 stretch run. He batted .296 in 56 games as the Yankees rallied for the flag and defeated the Dodgers in the Series, the one marked by Reggie Jackson's four straight home runs, three in the final game.

He hit only .184 in a backup role in that 1978 season and was batting .266 in 28 games in 1979 before he was traded to Cleveland.

He may or may not have been traded because of a scuffle he had with Yankee relief ace Rich Gossage, possibly the match of the two largest combatants in baseball history. Gossage was an intimidating fastball pitcher with a 100-mile-an-hour heater who wore a scary Fu Manchu mustache and topped out at about six foot three and 200 pounds. After a couple of punches and a lot of wrestling, Gossage wound up with a broken thumb. He was out of the action for three months.

The fact of their having fought at all was strange because Johnson and Gossage were both affable guys off the field though tough competitors in uniform. It was all caused by some silly, sarcastic kidding by Reggie Jackson, not only Mr. October but also King of the Needlers.

"Goose and I were good friends before the event, and we have remained good friends ever since," Johnson said. "I played 15 years in the big-leagues with a good career, and I don't want people thinking of me in that way."

Johnson said he was very upset only recently when some fan walked up to him at an outing and began relating details of the Gossage happening.

"He didn't know anything about me, he didn't know me, and he had no sense of my pride in my career. To talk about that was insulting. I just walked away," he said.

Johnson said he is still emotional about his days with the Yankees.

"That was the pinnacle of my career—two seasons and two World Series. That's pretty good," he said. "I loved all the guys. A great bunch. I guess my favorite was Catfish Hunter. He was a farmer, and we often talked about working the land. He understood what it was like."

Johnson was a wonderful addition to the Yankees in those winning days, on the field, with his power and versatility, and off the field with his friendliness and warm smile.

"Maybe they got rid of me because I went my own way," he said. "After the last game of the Series we were getting ready for a ticker-tape parade down Broadway in New York. The bus was loaded. I just got in my new car and drove off for the highway on my way to Texas. I just missed the ranch."

RON KLIMKOWSKI

R on Klimkowski, a tall righthander, joined the Yankees at the tag end of the 1969 season. This was three years after the Yankees had actually finished in 10th place in 1966 and long after the heroic Yankee names of Mickey Mantle, Whitey Ford, Yogi Berra and Roger Maris had passed from the Stadium scene.

It was in those CBS-owned rebuilding years that players came and went around the Bronx in hopes of returning to the glory of the 1940s, '50s and early '60s.

There were some prime-time players such as Mel Stottlemyre, Bobby Murcer, Roy White and Joe Pepitone, but there were also fringe big-leaguers keeping the Yankees at the back of the pack under second-tour skipper Ralph Houk.

"I always dreamed about playing for the Yankees," said Klimkowski. "When I was a little kid a friend of my mother's had a sewing business. One day she sent me a baseball uniform, just like a Yankee uniform, with a large No. 5 on it for Joe DiMaggio. I must have gone to school, ate and slept in that uniform for days."

On August 3, 1967, the Yankees traded famed catcher Elston Howard to the Boston Red Sox. The Yankees obtained a promising 23-year-old pitcher named Ron Klimkowski in the deal.

NEW YORK YANKEES

RON KLIMKOWSKI — PITCHER

SEASONS WITH YANKEES: 1969-70; 1972

Best Season with Yankees: 1970

Games: 45 • **Record: 6-7** • ERA: 2.65 • **Innings Pitched: 98 $^1/_3$** • Hits Allowed: 80 • **Strikeouts: 40** • Walks: 33

Howard became part of Boston's Impossible Dream team, the Boston club led by Triple Crown winner and future Hall of Famer Carl Yastrzemski into the World Series against the Cardinals. Of course, Bob Gibson won three games for the Cardinals, beat Jim Lonborg in the seventh game and led St. Louis to a 4-3 Series win. Once again, it was The Curse of the Bambino.

While Howard was playing in his 10th World Series, Klimkowski was dreaming his own impossible dream, finally wearing an adult Yankee uniform.

Ronald Bernard Klimkowski was born March 1, 1944, in Jersey City, New Jersey. The family soon moved to Queens, New York and later Westbury, Long Island, New York, where Klimkowski starred as a first baseman and pitcher.

In 1962 he was invited to a group workout of high school kids at the Polo Grounds in Manhattan where the fledgling New York Mets were on their way that year to a record 120 losses.

"There was one kid there who seemed to get all the attention. That was Ed Kranepool, who had been a big star in the Bronx at James Monroe High School. The Mets signed him and the rest of us were forgotten," Klimkowski said.

Klimkowski went off to Morehead State in Kentucky and again was a slugging first baseman as well as a hard-throwing pitcher. Another Yankee, the late Steve Hamilton, later became athletic director at Morehead State, his alma mater.

"After my second season at Morehead, the Red Sox scout, Bots Nikola, offered me $10,000 and some incentive bonuses to sign. He told me the Red Sox wanted me as a pitcher, and I should forget about first base," he said.

Klimkowski was sent to Waterloo, Iowa, and then to Winston-Salem, North Carolina. He pitched 221 innings that year with a 13-12 record and was moved to the Red Sox top club at Pittsfield, Massachusetts.

"I thought I was on my way to Boston when I was told I was traded for Elston Howard. That was pretty impressive. Later on, when I was with the Yankees, they traded me to Oakland for Felipe Alou. Some pretty good names for me, right?"

Klimkowski went to Binghamton in the Yankee organization where his catcher was Thurman Munson, moved the next year into a relief spot at Syracuse where he didn't give up an earned run and joined the Yankees for three games at the end of the 1969 season.

"The first batter I faced in the big leagues was Hall of Famer Al Kaline. I got him out and then gave up my first hit to Bill Freehan," Klimkowski said. "I still have that picture in my den of me facing Kaline for my first big-league appearance."

A week later Houk came to Klimkowski and told him he was starting against his old team, the Boston Red Sox, in Fenway Park.

He pitched eight scoreless innings against Boston before the Red Sox won the game in the 12th inning.

He started three games and relieved 42 times with a 6-7 record and a 2.65 ERA for the 1970 Yankees. His career mark was 8-12 with an impressive 2.90 ERA.

He was traded to Oakland and received a call from the A's boss, Charlie Finley, who told him to fly to California, join the team there and then fly on to the next series at Milwaukee.

"I was not about to do that," he said. "I took my time packing and told Finley I would join the club in Milwaukee. Rollie Fingers had been starting and relieving and they finally switched him to full-time relief pitching. That cut me out of a lot of innings," he said.

The A's, who would go on to win three straight World Series in 1972, 1973 and 1974, were swept in three games in the 1971 AL Championship Series by Baltimore.

"Catfish [Hunter] pitched the first game, Vida Blue started the second game and I was supposed to start the third game. At the last minute Dick Williams switched to [Diego] Segui, and I lost my chance at a playoff spot," he said.

In the spring of 1972, Klimkowski was doing his running on a wet field. His right knee gave out, he fell to the turf and his career was soon headed downhill.

The Yankees brought him back for 16 games with an 0-3 mark in 1972. He was soon released.

Klimkowski returned home, got into the automobile sales business where he sold Cadillacs to rich people in Great Neck, New York and settled in Syosset, New York.

He and his wife, Donna, are the parents of one daughter, Lindsay Morgan, 21, an outstanding five-foot-10 basketball player at New York Tech.

"I don't know if she will make the WNBA, but she has saved us a lot of money with her basketball scholarships," Klimkowski said.

After several years as an auto salesman, Klimkowski sold a car to a local stockbroker. He suggested Klimkowski try Wall Street. He worked as a stockbroker for five years, did well and soon joined a company that used computers to evaluate professional umpires.

"It put me back in the game, and I got to meet up with a lot of guys from the old days," he said. "Unfortunately the company downsized about a year ago so I'm not really doing anything now. I just watch a lot of games on television."

Klimkowski has a room in his house filled with old photos of his playing days, a White House visit with President Richard Nixon in 1969 and pictures with pals, Thurman Munson and Mike Hegan, his Yankee roommate.

"You know when you play with the Yankees, even as little time as I did, people always remember you. Wherever I go and introduce myself, people will say how they know my name and remember me pitching with the Yankees. They ask about some other guys on the team, [Mel] Stottlemyre, [Bobby] Murcer, Munson, you know—the name guys. I still think it's fun to talk about those guys and talk about the old days."

Klimkowski said he has been invited back to Yankee Stadium for a couple of Old Timer events and can still get a few tickets as an old Yankee when he wants to entertain some out-of-town friend at the Stadium.

"I didn't have a long career but I fulfilled my dream of playing for the Yankees. I had that little Yankee uniform with the No. 5 as a kid and I had that big uniform when I joined the Yankees in 1969," he said.

Klimkowski said he sometimes thinks that his career might have been different if he hadn't had the accident and his knee injury.

"You gotta have a good arm and good legs to pitch in the big-leagues," he said. "I had that for a while, and it was great fun. I'm on that list of all those guys who played for the Yankees—Babe Ruth, Lou Gehrig, Joe DiMaggio, Mickey Mantle and the rest. That will be something to show my grandchildren."

HECTOR
LOPEZ

In his first five full seasons with the Yankees from 1960 to 1964, Hector Lopez played in five World Series, won two championships in 1961 and 1962, played a lot of outfield when Mickey Mantle was hurt and Yogi Berra cut his eye with his sunglasses, hit a Series homer in 1961, had a Series career average of .286 and established his credentials as a living legend in his home country of Panama.

"They didn't have television in those days, but people gathered around the radio and listened to the games. My father was a salesman and spoke English as well as Spanish. He told everybody what was going on and what I was doing," Lopez said.

What he was doing during his 12-year career with the Kansas City A's and the New York Yankees was collecting 1,251 hits with a lifetime average of .269. He played on some of baseball's most glamorous teams, including the 1961 home run Yankees. He was a solid performer anywhere he was asked to play.

"Hector was never a spectacular player, but he was one of those guys you could always depend on when you needed him," said Ralph Houk, who was his manager and general manager in those pennant-winning seasons.

SEASONS WITH YANKEES: 1959-66

Best Season with Yankees: 1959

Games: 112 (as a Yankee) • **Batting Average: .283** • At-Bats: 406 • **Hits: 115** • Runs: 60 • **Home Runs: 16** • RBI: 69

Hector Headley Lopez Swainson, known as Hector Headley (his father's surname) Lopez in his playing career, was born in Colon, Panama on July 9, 1929. His father, Manuel, worked as a salesman throughout the area and provided a good home and plenty of food for the family.

"I started playing ball when I was 14 or 15 and was playing for a lot of the amateur teams around home. We were all Yankee fans because that was the team we heard the most about and listened to on the radio," he said.

He was signed by the old Philadelphia A's and joined the transferred Kansas City A's in 1955. He quickly established his big-league credentials with a .290 batting average as a third baseman under manager Lou Boudreau. The Kansas City team included several other players with past or future Yankee connections such as Joe DeMaestri, Enos Slaughter, Art Ditmar, Bobby Shantz, Vic Raschi and Clete Boyer.

Lopez proved his hitting skills through 1959 with the A's and played third, second and some outfield in Kansas City.

The Yankees had a warm and wonderful relationship with Kansas City, the former hometown of their best farm club, and seemed able to reach down into the KC roster when they needed help.

On May 26, 1959, Yankee GM George Weiss and manager Casey Stengel decided they needed some pitching help and another useful outfielder. They sent pitchers Tom Sturdivant, Johnny Kucks and infielder Jerry Lumpe to Kansas City for pitcher Ralph Terry and Hector Lopez.

The Yankees didn't win in 1959 (manager Al Lopez of Chicago denied old pal Stengel his second pennant in 11 seasons), but Hector Lopez started his Series streak in 1960.

"I was just excited to play ball with those Yankee teams," Lopez said. "I think the 1960 and 1961 teams may have been the best in baseball, ever. We had everything—power, pitching, great defense, depth and great leadership. It was fun to be on those teams."

Lopez's mother had moved to Brooklyn, and Hector moved in with her as soon as he came to New York. He commuted to Yankee Stadium by subway and enjoyed talking with Yankee fans as the subway trains neared the famous 161st station across from Yankee Stadium.

After his final season with the Yankees in 1966—a dreadful 10th-place finish for a team with aging players including Lopez at 37—the outfielder spent the next couple of years playing in the minor leagues with the Washington Senators organization. He played for Buffalo in 1968 and hoped to make the Senators as a backup outfielder under Ted Williams in 1969 at age 40. It never happened.

He and his wife, Claudette, set up residence in Hempstead, Long Island. They had four sons, two of whom died of illnesses, and now have six grandchildren, all residing in the New York area.

Lopez soon got a job with the recreation department of Hempstead. For 20 years he ran clinics, established a variety of programs, took youngsters to games at the Stadium, talked to school groups and clubs and contributed mightily to the positive reinforcement needed by underprivileged children.

"I enjoyed that very much. I loved working with kids," he said. "After a while, I decided it was time to move back to warmer weather."

Lopez established his home in the small town of Hudson, Florida, worked with Little League kids, did some fishing and enjoyed having time to relax. He also did some scouting for the Yankees in the Florida area and in Central and South America.

"I would go back to the Stadium every so often for an Old Timers game and I realized how much I missed being in the game," he said.

Yankee owner George Steinbrenner heard of Lopez's interest in returning to the game and hired him in 1991 to work as an outfield and hitting instructor with the Yankees rookie league team in the Gulf Coast league at Tampa.

"I worked with a lot of the kids on their way up," Lopez said. "There were always a few youngsters you knew were on their way to the big leagues."

Lopez said he remembered when Derek Jeter, the great Yankee shortstop, joined the club in 1992.

"As soon as you watched the kid play you knew he was something special," Lopez said. "He had all the moves and he was very confident on the field. He was a little raw with the glove and made a few errors, but he was willing to work hard. He would come out early, and I would hit him a lot of balls. He was very determined to get better. I'm not surprised at how good he got—one of the very best in the game."

Lopez commutes back and forth to the ballpark, just 45 minutes from his home, works with the youngsters before the game, watches a few innings and then drives back home for fun in the sun.

"I'm 74 years old and I'm still in pretty good shape. I enjoy being around these kids, and it is always thrilling to me when someone moves up the ladder and makes it big in New York," he said.

Hector Lopez has those five Yankee World Series experiences to tell the kids about and an impressive 12-year stay in the big-leagues. He is a very contented man.

"I don't know if all these good things would have happened if I stayed in Kansas City," he said. "When you play for the Yankees everybody knows your name. I was excited the first day I came to the Stadium and I am still excited when I come back."

STAN BAHNSEN

H e remembers that first moonlit night at Yankee Stadium in 1966 as if it was yesterday.

"I got to the Stadium about 2 or 3 in the morning, this kid from Iowa, nervous as hell, never having been in New York and now banging on the door of the clubhouse," said Stan Bahnsen.

Pete Sheehy, the clubhouse man for several generations who lived in the clubhouse when the team was at home, opened the door.

"I told him who I was and dropped my bag in a corner. He asked me if I wanted to see the Stadium and he took me down that ramp to the field. I walked up the dugout steps on this beautiful, clear night with a full moon lighting up the sky. This was the old Stadium, and the monuments were out in centerfield. I could see them from the grass as I walked on the field. I had to pinch myself to believe where I was. Even now, after all these years, I can still feel that emotion."

After a back injury in 1967, Bahnsen came back to stay with the Yankees in 1968, lighting up the struggling franchise like that full moon, making 34 starts, pitching 10 complete games, winning 17 games against 12 losses, turning in a 2.05 ERA and being clearly marked for stardom. It earned him the American League Rookie of the Year award.

SEASONS WITH YANKEES: 1966-71

Best Season with Yankees: 1968 (Rookie of the Year)

Games: 37 • Record: 17-12 (sixth in wins in AL) • ERA: 2.05 (sixth in AL) • Innings Pitched: 267 1/3 (sixth in AL) • Hits Allowed: 216 • Strikeouts: 162 • Walks: 68

He won 115 games in his first eight seasons with New York, Chicago and Oakland, including a 21-game winning season with the White Sox in 1972.

"Wilbur Wood, the knuckleballer, was on that team and he often pitched on two days' rest. Chuck Tanner [the Chicago manager] often asked me if I wanted to follow Wilbur with two days or wait my turn out with five days of rest. I usually went for the two days of rest, and as a hard thrower I think I felt it later on in my career. I started 41 games that year and 42 the next," Bahnsen said.

Stanley Raymond Bahnsen was born December 15, 1944, in Council Bluffs, Iowa. He starred on local amateur teams around Iowa and won a scholarship to the University of Nebraska.

"A Yankee scout, Joe McDermott, had watched me for about three years and after my sophomore season at Nebraska he came up with a bonus offer. I signed in 1966, got to the Stadium at the end of the year and was pitching regularly two years later," he said.

In his first turn with the Yankees in 1966 and in spring training the next season he got to meet many of the aging Yankee stars: Mickey Mantle, Whitey Ford, Elston Howard, Roger Maris and so many other names going downhill at that stage.

"Mickey and Elston and Roger took me out to dinner one night. There I was sitting in some fancy restaurant with these guys after collecting their baseball cards just a few years earlier," he said.

Bahnsen said he even got Mantle to sign a baseball for him that still sits in a prominent place in his home in Pompano Beach, Florida that he now shares with his second wife, Cindy. He and his first wife, Connie, had one son, Brent, now 26.

"Later on I got into the promotion business and I saw the value of some of these signed things. I was at a show when they sold a signed Joe DiMaggio Yankee shirt for $75,000. Boy, was I sorry I didn't get him to sign something for me," Bahnsen said.

After the 1971 season, the Yankees, desperate for a third baseman, traded Bahnsen to the White Sox for third baseman Rich McKinney, a deal that would haunt Yankee General Manager Lee MacPhail the rest of his career.

Bahnsen won 21, 18 and 12 games for the White Sox before moving on to the Oakland A's. He went to Montreal in 1977 and finished up with California and Philadelphia in 1982.

The handsome righthander compiled a big-league mark of 146-149 over 16 seasons with an impressive 3.61 ERA in 574 games.

"I was offered a triple A job by the Phillies when I was finished, but I had enough travel. I decided to go back home to Florida, play some golf and relax," he said.

Bahnsen had done some promotional work for Arrow Shirts while he was playing in New York and continued making appearances for them. He soon started his own promotional company, putting theme cruises together for cruise lines and sponsoring autograph shows.

"I had Hall of Famers like Bob Feller and Stan Musial make appearances for us, and I had current stars like Jason Giambi and Al Leiter with us on some of the cruises. All they do is sign autographs for half an hour and then enjoy a week's cruise," he said.

Bahnsen did some American Legion ball coaching around home and even spent a summer in Holland working with some local teams.

"They like baseball there. They have a few Americans on the teams but most of them are locals," he said.

"The teams weren't very good because all the best athletes in Holland play soccer."

Bahnsen got his top pitching salary up to $275,000 a year in the days mostly before free agency, played with a couple of contenders, made it to the divisional playoffs with Montreal in 1981 when the Dodgers beat them and had an impressive career.

"The Yankees still invite me back for a lot of the Old Timer games, and I get to see a lot of the guys through the promotional events I do," he said.

"I'm still friendly with old teammates like Jim Lyttle and Steve Whitaker who live in the area."

All in all, a strong career and a successful professional life have made Stan Bahnsen a satisfied man. Only a pennant along the way could have made it better.

JOE
DeMAESTRI

I n the den of Joe DeMaestri's handsome home in Novato, California—in the Mill Valley just outside of San Francisco—pictures,
bats, old uniforms and gloves fill most of the space.

"We call it my Memorial Room," laughed DeMaestri. "My wife
says the only thing we don't do in there is light candles."

DeMaestri and his wife of 52 years, Margo, have furnished the
room with pictures of the World Series Yankee teams of 1960 and
1961. There are shots of DeMaestri playing in the Stadium, and the
bats and balls he used in his two Yankee seasons with two of baseball's
best teams ever.

DeMaestri was the backup shortstop to Tony Kubek for those
two seasons, and they were very close friends.

"We used to live in the old Stadium Motor Lodge up the hill
from the Stadium and we would walk to the ballpark together every
home game," he said.

In 1960, DeMaestri got into 49 games for the Yankees as manager Casey Stengel maneuvered his lineup.

"Casey knew how to keep everybody involved," DeMaestri said.
"He often had Yogi in the outfield with Mickey [Mantle] and Roger
[Maris] and then he would take Yogi out and put Kubek in left field

JOE DEMAESTRI
INFIELD
YANKEES

SEASONS WITH YANKEES: 1960-61

Best Season with Yankees: 1960

Games: 49 • **Batting Average: .229** • At-Bats: 35 • **Hits: 8** •
Runs: 8 • **Home Runs: 0** • RBI: 2

in a close game and I would go to shortstop. I got a lot of playing time and felt like a big part of the club."

He got into four games in the 1960 World Series with one hit in two tries for a .500 Series average. That was the Series won by Pittsburgh on Bill Mazeroski's homer over Yogi Berra's head in left field.

"Everybody knew we were a better ball club. We scored all the runs [55 to Pittsburgh's 27] but they won the seventh game. That was all that really mattered. I remember Mickey sitting on the training table just crying like a baby. It hurt so much."

At the age of 32, he played his final season in the big-leagues with the Yankees in 1961. DeMaestri played 30 games with just a .146 average and retired at the end of the year.

"Actually I played two more seasons in the big-leagues than I expected to," he said. "It was only because I was traded to the Yankees. I had made up my mind after the 1959 season that I was going home. I had a family to be concerned about and I also had a beer distributorship business that my father ran and wanted me to take over."

A persuasive call from Yankee general manager George Weiss and a salary raise to $21,000 convinced DeMaestri to come to New York.

"It was the greatest decision of my baseball life. I had only played on bad teams up to then. The Yankees were different. They didn't know what losing meant. I remember the first few days I was there. I was dressing next to Gil McDougald. 'Hey, don't screw with my money,' McDougald said. They just looked at the World Series money as part of their annual salary."

Joseph Paul DeMaestri was born December 9, 1928 in San Francisco. He was a baseball All-Star at Tamalpais High School in Mill Valley. His grandson, Joe III, known as Jay DeMaestri, was a basketbAll-Star at the same school in 2003.

DeMaestri, a smooth shortstop and a decent contact hitter, was signed by the Boston Red Sox in 1947. He was drafted by the Chicago White Sox and made the big club in 1951.He played one year in Chicago before moving on to the St. Louis Browns and then the Philadelphia A's in 1953. He had his best year in the big-leagues with the A's with a .255 average in 111 games that season. He was the regular

shortstop for the downtrodden A's—now moved to Kansas City—
through 1959.

"Losing got a little tiresome," he said. "I figured it was over."

Then came the two dream seasons with the Yankees.

"What was difficult was staying in shape with the Yankees. I
had played every day up until that. With the Yankees I might go three
or four weeks without getting into a game."

The six foot, 170 pounder was often told by Stengel and then
Ralph Houk to always be ready.

"I was talking to Tony Kubek a few years back and he reminded
me why I didn't play much. He said nobody ever seemed to get hurt
on those good Yankee teams," DeMaestri said.

DeMaestri finished with 11 years in the big-leagues, a .236 lifetime average and strong defense at shortstop, second base and occasionally at third base.

"I still keep myself in pretty good shape," said DeMaestri, who
retired from the beer business in 1990. "I get into a lot of these charity golf tournaments around here and I see a lot of guys from the old
days. I still wear that 1961 championship ring and a lot of the golfers
like to stare at that."

Joe and Margo DeMaestri are the parents of three children, have
eight grandchildren and now have four great grandchildren.

"Most of the kids are here in the San Francisco area so I enjoy
visiting with them. I watch my grandson play basketball. I still watch
some of the Yankee games on television and I watch the Oakland
games. I'm not much interested in the other teams I played with in
those days."

Only two of his 11 big-league seasons were with the Yankees,
but DeMaestri says those two years really changed his professional
life and gave him an identification back home he never would have
had without that Yankee logo.

A World Series ring can work wonders for old ballplayers.

TOMMY JOHN

He is one of the legendary figures in the game: 26 years in the big leagues, 288 wins, a lifetime 3.34 ERA, 760 games, three 20-win seasons, four All-Star games, three World Series appearances and contributions to six winning teams.

The fact that Tommy John is not a Cooperstown bust in Baseball's Hall of Fame is one of the embarrassments of baseball.

Add his playing performance to the fact that he was Los Angeles surgeon Dr. Frank Jobe's first reconstructive elbow surgery—now copyrighted as Tommy John Surgery in medical books.

"When I had that surgery in 1974, Dr. Jobe told me it was very experimental," recalled John. "He said if I didn't have it I would never pitch again. If I did have it and it didn't work I would never pitch again. If I did have it and it worked, well, he couldn't even guess."

After winning 13 games for the Los Angeles Dodgers that year, he sat out the 1975 season while working on his recovery. He was 10-10 with the Dodgers in 1976, earning baseball's Comeback Player of the Year award, and then won 20 games and 17 games for Los Angeles in the next two seasons as he helped the Dodgers to the pennants.

Then he became a free agent, signed with the Yankees, won 21 games in 1979 and 22 in 1980. Even Dr. Jobe was surprised.

YANKEES

TOMMY JOHN

SEASONS WITH YANKEES: 1979-82; 1986-89

Best Season with Yankees: 1979 (All Star; 2nd in Cy Young voting)

Games: 37 • Record: 21-9 (second in AL in wins; seventh in won-loss percentage) • ERA: 2.96 (second in AL) • Innings Pitched: 276 1/3 (second in AL) • Hits Allowed: 268 • Strikeouts: 111 • Walks: 65 • Complete Games: 17 (second in AL)

"At last count there were over a hundred guys in the big leagues who had the surgery and were pitching. Actually most of them pitch better than they did before, because their speed increases. Dr. Jobe always said your arm got stronger as you used it more," John said.

When John broke into the big-leagues in 1963 with Cleveland he matched up with Warren Spahn, the game's winningest lefthander, in a spring game. Spahn was always an advocate of throwing every day to keep an arm loose. He even did it in the bitter cold of his Oklahoma home.

"I was just thrilled to be out there against him," said John. "Pitchers batted then and I lined a single off the great Warren Spahn. Then he nearly picked me off first base. He was some competitor."

Thomas Edward John was born May 22, 1943, in Terre Haute, Indiana. He was signed out of high school by the Cleveland Indians and made it to the big-leagues in 1963. He was 0-2 and 2-9 with Cleveland before being moved to the White Sox in a deal involving Rocky Colavito. He established his big-league credentials in Chicago with two 14-win seasons, stayed there through 1971 and moved to the Dodgers in a trade for super slugger Dick Allen.

He had six impressive seasons with the Dodgers, including a 1978 World Series win before moving to New York in a big free-agent signing.

John had eight seasons in New York in two separate tours and became one of the team's most popular players. Despite all the turmoil around George Steinbrenner's Yankees, John always seemed to keep his head.

John and wife, Sally, mother of their four children, gained much attention and sympathy when their third child, Travis, then only three years old, fell from their apartment window in New Jersey.

His life hung in the balance for many days, but doctors pulled him through. Travis is now a healthy 24-year-old, who played baseball in college, and now works in the sporting goods business.

"Actually I'm thinking of going into business with Travis after I get my degree in exercise science. We can open a shop with exercise workout equipment and all the goods a customer might need," John said.

John beat the Dodgers in the 1981 World Series for the Yankees. He was traded to California in 1982, pitched for Oakland and came back to the Yankees in 1986. His career ended in some bitterness in 1989 when he wasn't ready to go.

"I could still pitch," insisted John, who was then 46 years old. "Sid Thrift [Yankee GM] and Dallas Green [Yankee manager] called me into the office and said George wanted me to move on with my career. I didn't quite know what that meant."

John looked at a few pitching opportunities, including one in St. Louis with Whitey Herzog, but finally decided 26 years with that pitching toe plate was enough.

He got a broadcasting job in Minnesota—quite a coup for a guy who had to conquer a stutter—and spent five years there before coming back to New York as a color analyst on the televised Yankee games.

He moved to Charlotte, North Carolina when the White Sox hired him as their radio color analyst for the Charlotte Knights and also used him as director of community relations.

"I guess I still missed being on the field," John said. "In 2002 Omar Minaya [Montreal GM] called me and asked if I was interested in getting back on the field as a pitching coach. I jumped at the chance and worked with the kids in Harrisburg. In 2003 I was selected as the pitching coach for the Edmonton Trappers, the Expos Triple A club."

John said that the Montreal connection really opened up new opportunities for him.

"A lot of the kids I worked with in Harrisburg and in Edmonton have moved up to the big club," he said. "I think with my pitching experience and this coaching I am ready for a big-league pitching coach job. I know the Yankees will make a change after the 2004 season and maybe other clubs will have openings."

At the age of 60, John has lost none of his enthusiasm or pitching acumen. He would make a wonderful addition to any team. If a pitcher happened to come up with elbow problems, he could also explain Tommy John surgery better than any doctor.

Where Have You Gone?

HAL
RENIFF

Hal Reniff was the kind of guy who never showed much excitement about playing in the big leagues, even when he was pitching for one of baseball's most glorious teams, the homer-happy 1961 Yankees.

"I just went out there and did my job the best I could," he said. "When the game was over, I came in, took my shower, got dressed and walked out into a different world."

He never bragged about his big-league connections or showed off his World Series rings and now—more than 40 years after those Yankee Series days—few friends around his home in Ontario, California talk with him about his Yankee time.

"That was then and this is now," Reniff said.

Reniff said he hardly ever goes to a baseball card show or appears at charity golf tournaments just to be connected again with his past life.

"It's just too much of a hassle to travel now. You have to get on a plane after sitting in the airport for two hours, fly to New York or New Jersey, sign a few autographs, listen to fans say dumb things about your career and collect a thousand or two thousand dollars. Somebody might get goofy about the 1961 Yankees, and I just want to walk away," he said.

HAL RENIFF
PITCHER
YANKEES

SEASONS WITH YANKEES: 1961-67

Best Season with Yankees: 1963

Games: 48 • **Record: 4-3** • ERA: 2.62 • **Saves: 18 (sixth in AL)** • Innings Pitched: 89 $^1/_3$ • **Hits Allowed: 63** • Strikeouts: 56 • **Walks: 42**

Reniff was a solid relief pitcher on that 1961 Yankee team, anchored by the M and M boys as Roger Maris hit 61 homers to break the old Babe Ruth record and Mickey Mantle hit 54 before falling out of the home run race because of an injury.

The relief star that year—the Mariano Rivera of his time—was Luis Arroyo, a screwball pitcher with incredible control. Arroyo won 15 games for the Yankees and saved another 29 games, one of the most remarkable relief marks in the history of the game. He pitched in 65 games.

Reniff appeared in 25 games, had a 2-0 mark and saved two games. Two years later he would save 18 games for the 1963 Yankees as the team won its fourth straight pennant on the way to another five wins in a row with two Series titles.

"Ralph Houk was the manager when I came to the Yankees in 1961. I had been a starter in the minors and done well. That spring he came to me and said he wanted to make me a relief pitcher. I didn't want that. Relief pitchers didn't make any money in those days. He said it was relief pitching or back to the minors, so I gave in," Reniff said.

Harold Eugene Reniff was born in Warren, Ohio on July 2, 1938. His father was a steelworker, and when the construction industry dried up in Ohio he moved the family to California during the post-war boom of the late 1940s and 1950s.

"I started in Little League out there and played PONY, American Legion, high school—just about everything. Kids in California have such an edge over everybody else because they just play so many damn games," he said.

Reniff was signed by Yankee scout Deacon Jones for less than $4,000.

"They had that stupid bonus rule then if you signed for over four you had to stay with the big club. Then they changed the rules and I was competing against guys who had signed for 50, 60, 75 thousand dollars and none of them were as good as me," he said.

He won 20 games as a starter at Modesto, California, and came to the Yankee camp in St. Petersburg in 1961 with high hopes of making Houk's rotation. That ended when Houk decided his six foot, 215 pounder—called Porky by his teammates—would better serve the club from the bullpen.

"I made the team and enjoyed all the guys. I was especially close to Roger [Maris] because we were a lot alike. We just did our jobs and went home. We didn't like the media fuss. Nobody ever had as much pressure in the game as Roger did that year," Reniff said.

The Yankees won the pennant in 1961, 1962 and 1963. In 1964 the team—under new manager Yogi Berra with Houk moved upstairs as GM—won again. They lost the World Series in seven games to the Cardinals. Yogi was fired the day after the Series ended.

"I think the Yankees changed forever after that. CBS bought the team, and it was all about money. The Yankee spirit, the history, the pride, seemed to be gone. After 1964 it was all about business," Reniff said.

Reniff was sold to the Mets in 1967. His seven-year, big-league career was soon over with a 21-23 mark and a 3.27 ERA in 276 games.

"I was having some circulatory problems in my shoulder, but the Yankees re-signed me and sent me to their Syracuse club. I thought I could get back to the big leagues. Lee MacPhail was the Yankee general manager by then and he was the most honest front office man I ever dealt with," Reniff said.

Reniff pitched well in Syracuse and had been most successful against Winnipeg, the Montreal farm club. GM Jim Fanning of Montreal wanted to bring Reniff to his club as a late-inning reliever.

"One day Fanning called me up and said the Yankees wouldn't let me go. I called MacPhail, and he told me Ralph, who was managing again, thought I deserved another shot with the Yankees. I had a good year in Syracuse in 1971 and then they released me in 1972. I never got back to the big leagues, which would have increased my pension by a lot. That made me angry," he said.

Reniff, who was divorced and had two children, stayed in Syracuse, did some broadcasting for the Chiefs, worked in a car dealership and eventually moved back to California.

"I play a little golf now with some old pals. I recently played with Ralph Terry, an old teammate, who was on that senior tour. I have fun when I get out there but I don't look for that. I stay home most of the time and just watch television," he said.

Reniff said he hasn't been back for Old Timers days in years and doesn't really miss it.

"As I get older it doesn't mean anything any more. Who cares that I played with the Yankees? I really don't talk about baseball. I have other things on my mind now," he said.

He was a valuable relief pitcher on four Yankee pennant winners in his seven big-league years, but he saw baseball as just another job. No different, emotionally, than his broadcasting jobs or car selling.

"I never got excited about playing baseball then," he said. "I ain't gonna change. I don't get excited talking about it now."

BRIAN DOYLE

He had a four-year career as a backup infielder with a lifetime .161 average, but Brian Doyle picked the right time to hit his peak, the 1978 American League Championship Series against Kansas City and the 1978 World Series against the Dodgers.

Doyle, playing second base in place of injured regular Willie Randolph, batted .286 in the ALCS won by the Yankees in four games and batted .438 in the Series won by the Yankees four games to two after the Dodgers won the first two games.

Bucky Dent, who had helped get the Yankees to the Series with his famous (or infamous) home run—depending on which side of the Charles River in Boston one lived—against the Red Sox in the playoff, hit .417 in the Series.

The World Series MVP was soon to be announced after the last game and Yankee catcher Thurman Munson shouted across the clubhouse to Doyle. "Brian, did you win it?"

Doyle could only shake his head because the winner had not yet been announced.

"Then a PR guy came over to me and said to follow him with Bucky over to a side room where the press was hanging out. They would make the announcement there. I got into the room, we both

SEASONS WITH YANKEES: 1978-80

Best Season with Yankees: 1980

Games: 34 • **Batting Average:** .173 • At-Bats: 75 • **Hits:** 13 •
Runs: 8 • **Home Runs: 1** • RBI: 5

sat at a table and the PR guy announced that Bucky Dent was the World Series MVP. I didn't feel badly. I had just had a great Series on a winning team," Doyle said.

Doyle's career had begun in the Texas organization, and he was traded to the Yankees for Sandy Alomar. He made the Yankees as a backup infielder in 1978 with a smooth glove and great knowledge of the game.

In 1980 he was sent to Oakland for pitcher Mike Morgan and ended his big-league career after the 1981 season with 110 big-league games and that .161 average. He was only 26 years old.

"The last year I was with Oakland I was making a double play, and Otto Velez, a strong runner, was coming into the base. He threw up his hands to avoid the ball as I threw to first and he knocked me over. I landed on my right shoulder, separated it badly and was finished. I signed with Toronto and later Cleveland and even coached in the big leagues with Cleveland. I just couldn't throw any more," he said.

Brian Reed Doyle was born in Glasgow, Kentucky, on January 26, 1955. He was 11 minutes older than his twin brother, Blake, and 11 years younger than his brother Denny Doyle, an eight-year big-leaguer with the Phillies, Angels and Red Sox.

"We grew up in Cave City, Kentucky, a town of 1800 people. My father, Robert, was a carpenter and also worked as a janitor at our Caverna High School where we all attended. We were all wild about baseball," he said.

He was only five years old when he began playing catch with his father and older brother who was already a town baseball star.

Doyle joined the Yankees out of spring training in 1978 but got little playing time behind Randolph until the last few weeks of the season.

"I wasn't nervous when I took over. We were in a tough pennant race, but I had played a lot of baseball by then. I was ready," he said.

Manager Bob Lemon showed a lot of confidence in Doyle in those final weeks of the season, into the playoff against Boston, the ALCS against Kansas City and the World Series. Doyle was steady with the glove and had a great ALCS and Series with the bat.

"I guess the only time I was nervous was when I walked on the field in Boston for the playoff. My brother Denny had played in the

1975 World Series with Boston and when I stood out there in the same spot I could feel those goose bumps all over my body," he said.

Doyle was on the bench after being hit for by Jim Spencer in the seventh inning when Bucky Dent hit that three-run homer off Mike Torrez. The Yankees scored four runs that inning to take a 4-2 lead they would never lose in the 5-4 win.

"I think every guy jumped up and banged his head against the top of the dugout. We came into the game with a lot of confidence and had so much confidence after the homer that we would win it with [Ron] Guidry and Goose [Gossage] going for us the rest of the way," he said.

That winter, Brian, Denny and Blake opened a small baseball academy in Winter Haven to teach youngsters from five years old and up how to play the game. Thousands of youngsters have passed through the school in the last 25 years.

The cost for instruction is $595 a week for local youngsters living at home or $799 a week with hotel and meals for boys coming from out of the area.

"We also have a three-week program in the summer for $3,800 with complete big-league facilities, training rooms, clubhouse men, intense all-day instruction, traveling games and top-notch equipment," he said.

Doyle and his wife of 30 years, Connie, have two grown children and one grandchild. They make their home in Winter Haven near the academy.

Doyle said more than 50 graduates of the school have moved into professional baseball with so many others winning college scholarships after their skills were improved at the Academy.

"We had this one kid a few years back," said Doyle. "He was 14 years old when he came to us. He fielded a couple of balls, and I told him he would be a big-league shortstop. That was Walt Weiss."

Doyle said the students often ask for autographs, stare at the big-league pictures he has on the walls and ask about that famous 1978 playoff game against the Red Sox.

"The school has been a great success. I think we were really helped by me being with the Yankees and playing in one of the most famous games ever," he said.

Doyle often shows off his 1978 World Series ring. He reminds his youngsters that working hard in baseball can lead to great rewards.

DAVE
RIGHETTI

L ou Gehrig delivered his touching farewell on July 4, 1939, the legendary Yankee connection with the nation's Independence Day birthday.

George Steinbrenner, born July 4, 1930, often marked his birthday at Yankee Stadium after acquiring the club in 1973.

However, not until a hot, hazy afternoon in the Bronx in 1983 had the Fourth of July taken on such an on-field element of historic significance.

On that afternoon a 24-year-old lefthander from San Jose, California struck out one of the game's greatest contact hitters, Wade Boggs, later a World Series Yankee, as the final batter in a no-hitter against the hated rival Red Sox.

Righetti's reward for the nine-inning classic contest was a spot in the Yankees bullpen the next year under new manager Yogi Berra after reliever Rich [Goose] Gossage took his 100-mile-an-hour fastball to San Diego.

Only four other Yankee pitchers before him had ever delivered no-hitters for the Yankees: George Mogridge in 1917 against Boston, Sad Sam Jones against Philadelphia in 1923, Monte Pearson against Cleveland in 1938 and Allie Reynolds twice in 1951 against Cleveland and Boston.

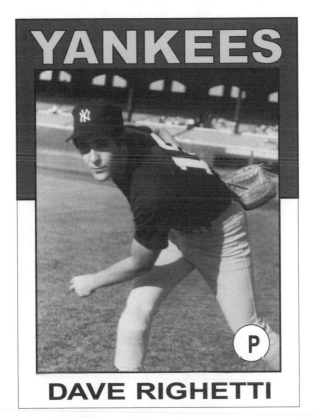

YANKEES

DAVE RIGHETTI

SEASONS WITH YANKEES: 1979-90

Best Season with Yankees: 1986 (Rolaids Relief Award; 10th in MVP voting; fourth in Cy Young voting)

Games: 74 • **Record: 8-8** • ERA: 2.45 • **Saves: 46 (first in AL)** • Innings Pitched: 106 $^2/_3$ • **Hits Allowed: 88** • Strikeouts: 83 • **Walks: 35**

New skipper Berra remembered the second one by Reynolds quite well. He had dropped a spinning pop foul hit by Ted Williams for the final out before Reynolds got Williams to pop up again to Berra for the last out of the second no-hitter.

Righetti's final pitch was just as dramatic with a hard slider to Boggs, a left-handed hitter, known for getting 200 hits almost every year and rarely striking out.

"I couldn't imagine that Boggs would swing and miss," admitted Righetti, now the pitching coach of the San Francisco Giants, when he talked about his 20-year-old no-hitter over the phone from San Francisco in 2003.

Catcher Butch Wynegar grabbed the final pitch and raced to the mound. Righetti had flung his arms into the air as the packed Stadium house roared but soon settled into a more composed manner in deference to his learned Yankee tradition of modesty in conduct and reverence for the past.

"I wish I had just let it go and enjoyed myself more," Righetti admitted in 2003.

Righetti was 14-8 that season with a 3.44 ERA in 31 starts. At the age of 24, in his seventh professional season as a starter, his career seemed unlimited and exciting.

Then the Yankee brass went to work. Gossage had moved on to San Diego after six sparkling save seasons in New York (150 saves including the October 2, 1978 save in the playoff against Boston) and the bullpen hole was huge.

A few names were tossed around by Steinbrenner's "baseball people" until the idea came forward that Dave Righetti, the no-hit starter, could do the job with his crackling fastball, sharp slider and excellent control.

Berra had always believed that a pitching staff is built from the back end, relievers being more important than starters.

Righetti went on to save 223 games in the next seven seasons through 1990. He never stopped thinking about his baseball life as a starting pitcher in all those years.

"I reconciled myself with it but there are definitely second thoughts and doubts," he said. "I had doubts as early as the next year. I understood why they did it and what it was about. I took it as an honor that they would trust me with the job."

David Allen Righetti was born in San Jose, California on November 28, 1958. He was a star at Pioneer High School in San Jose and won a scholarship to San Jose City College. He was named Junior College Player of the Year in 1977 before signing with the Yankees.

Righetti came from a baseball family with his father, Leo, in the Yankees minor league system for several years, and his brother, Steve, in the Texas organization. He followed the San Francisco Giants with Willie McCovey as his favorite Giant.

He won 11 games in Asheville, North Carolina, in his first pro season and moved quickly through the Yankee chain with a 1979 stop at the Stadium before establishing himself in 1981 with an 8-4 mark.

Righetti beat Milwaukee twice in the 1981 Division Championship Series, won a game against Oakland in the ALCS but was then hit hard in his only Series start against the Dodgers.

The handsome, smiling six-foot-four 220-pounder known as "Rags" by teammates and friends soon became a popular figure in New York nightlife as one of the team's eligible bachelors.

He won 11 games in 1982, won 14 with the no-hitter in 1983 and then collected 162 saves with a high of 46 in 1986 over the next seven seasons out of the pen.

The American League 1981 Rookie of the Year had clearly established himself as one of the game's great relief pitchers by the end of the decade. The Yankees, in the meantime, went nowhere in their down cycle with managers being changed rapidly by Steinbrenner and team finishes no better than second.

Righetti decided to move on to San Francisco as a free agent in 1991. He saved 24 games for the Giants that year. He spent three more years in Candlestick before short stops in Oakland, Toronto and Chicago. In 16 seasons he was 82-79 with 252 saves and a career 3.46 ERA.

He stayed out of baseball for a few years, played golf, thought about his starting career that got away, and enjoyed staying home with wife Kandice and their triplets, born in 1991.

The Giants asked him if he was interested in getting back in the game in 1999 as a roving minor league pitching instructor. He was named the team's pitching coach the following season and has seen his pitchers post impressive ERAs over the four seasons from 2000 to 2003.

He still thinks about the no-hitter 20 years later and his lost starting career.

"People always remember the game and where they were that day," he said.

"I still get a lot of mail, especially from military members who heard it on Armed Forces radio. "Those were the coolest letters to get."

He can't complain about a wonderful 16-year big-league pitching career. The no-hitter was the highlight. Righetti was only 24 when he did that. Nolan Ryan had seven no-hitters. Could lifelong starter Righetti have threatened that mark?

TEX
CLEVENGER

T ruman Eugene Clevenger was born July 9, 1932, in Visalia, California.

"My parents were from Missouri but they were rock-hard Republicans. I know that I wasn't named after Harry Truman. I never could find out where the name came from. It might have been a long lost family name, but when I was a kid nobody seemed to know so pretty soon I forgot about it," Clevenger said.

His baseball nickname of Tex, as he was known for his eight years of big-league pitching, is a little easier to explain.

"I was with the Red Sox organization in the early 1950s, and Johnny Pesky—everybody called him Needle Nose—was an infielder with the club. I was tall and pretty lanky in those days and had sort of a sidearm motion. He saw me pitch and he said that I pitched like one of his great old teammates, Tex Hughson. He began calling me Tex and it stuck."

Clevenger said the nickname was always good for a story, especially when his teammates from Texas would come up and ask him what part of the Lone Star State he was from.

"When I told the guys I was from California and had never been to Texas they looked at me kind of funny. It was always good for

SEASONS WITH YANKEES: 1961-62

Best Season with Yankees: 1962

Games: 21 • **Record: 2-0** • ERA: 2.84 • **Innings Pitched: 38** •
Hits Allowed: 36 • **Strikeouts: 11** • Walks: 17

a laugh. I used to say that it was better than being from Louisiana. Then the players would call me Louise," he said.

Clevenger was signed out of high school by the Red Sox and made it to the big club in 1954 with a 2-4 mark. He was in the minors the next season and then moved over to Washington in 1956 for a five-year stay with the team identified by the line, "First in war, first in peace and last in the American League."

"Washington was a bad ball club, and I didn't get a lot of support there. I couldn't make much money pitching for the Senators but at least I was in the big leagues," he said.

Clevenger was 29-31 with Washington before being selected by the expansion Los Angeles Angels in 1961 under new manager Bill Rigney and the easy ownership of movie cowboy star Gene Autry.

"I was making $14,000 that year and I sat down with Autry and GM Fred Haney to talk about my contract. I was determined to make more money and I told them Washington had promised me $2,500 more for the next season. I made a strong case for a raise, and Autry and Haney didn't say a thing. Finally Haney said, 'What the hell do you think we got you for? We want you to pitch for us.' That meant they'd give me the raise, and I felt pretty good about that," he said.

Clevenger got into 12 games with a 2-1 mark for the 1961 Angels through early May. The Angels were playing the Yankees one day, and Yogi Berra, baseball's super gossip, came up to him, slapped him on the bottom and said, "You're gonna be with us."

"I didn't know anything about it and I thought Yogi was kidding. The next day they called me and told me I was going to the Yankees. What a thrill that was," he said.

Former Yankee Bob Cerv, who would play an important role in the home run chase of Roger Maris and Mickey Mantle as a pal of both sluggers in that 1961 season, was traded back to the Yankees along with Clevenger for Ryne Duren, Lee Thomas and Johnny James.

"Ralph [Houk] used me strictly as a reliever, and I got a lot of work. It was just exciting to be part of that Yankee team, and I'll never forget that last day when Roger hit the home run to break the Ruth record. Nobody ever forgets that day," he said.

He was on the Yankees World Series winners in 1961 and 1962 but wasn't used in either Series. But he can still show off his World Series rings to friends and family.

"After that year they sent me out to the Richmond farm club. I was with Mel Stottlemyre on that team, and you could see that he was going to be something special. Great stuff and great control and a lot of poise for a kid," Clevenger said.

Clevenger pitched his final season in Birmingham and then decided to go home to California—not Texas—and pick up the rest of his life.

He ended his big-league career with a 36-37 mark in 307 games with a 4.18 ERA in eight seasons.

"I got into the insurance business near home and stayed in that from 1964 to 1972. Then the bottom sort of fell out, and I became a farmer for a few years," he said.

Clevenger later took a job with a Ford dealer near his home and finally bought the distributorship of Ford-Lincoln-Mercury in Porterville in the early 1990s.

A phone call to the dealership called Clevenger Ford—which Tex lives near—can put a caller in touch with Mr. Truman Clevenger.

"The people who know I played baseball call me Tex. The others call me Truman or Mr. Clevenger," he said.

Clevenger and his wife, Donna, have two children, two grandchildren and two great grandchildren.

"Our kids live in Louisiana, and we get down to visit with them every so often. I'm just glad I wasn't raised there and called Louise. Can you imagine standing on the mound and hearing some fan yell out, 'Get 'em out, Louise.' That would be something," he said.

Clevenger, who played at about 180 pounds, saw his weight climb to 250 pounds several years back. He had some health problems and had to undergo surgery. He made a complete recovery and now keeps himself at a manageable 230 pounds.

"I sponsor a charity golf tournament out here every year, and we get a lot of guys from our area. Joe DeMaestri, a 1961 teammate, always plays in it, and I had Dave Righetti and Bobby Jones, who used to pitch for the Mets and a few other big-leaguers. I even had Joe DiMaggio one year. That was something."

Clevenger works a full schedule at the automobile dealership, answers questions about Mickey and Roger for a while before selling a car, visits often with his family and gets on the golf course almost every weekend.

"I don't follow much baseball now. I get interested in the play-offs. Once in a while I tell a few stories about the old days to my golfing buddies. If you ever played for the Yankees," he said, "your name has a way of staying alive. I was pretty lucky to get traded over to the Yankees at just the right time. I made the team picture and keep it hung in the office."

GEORGE ZEBER

He had only two years in the big leagues with 28 games, 71 at-bats and a lifetime .296 average. He also has what Ernie Banks and so many others never had, a World Series ring from his time with the 1977 world champion Yankees.

"I had some ups and downs in baseball," said George Zeber, "but I look back at it all today with a pretty satisfied feeling."

Zeber—a handsome, trim backup infielder to Bucky Dent, Willie Randolph and Graig Nettles on those 1977 Yankees—played for Billy Martin's only Series winner that year.

"Billy didn't intimidate me," said Zeber. "I had been around baseball eight or nine years by the time I got to the Yankees, so I had seen just about everything you can see in the game by then."

Martin was known for his temper tantrums, but ironically he seemed to save his best outburst for the stars on the team—Reggie Jackson, Thurman Munson, Lou Piniella, Catfish Hunter—and not for the underused backup players like Zeber.

George William Zeber was born in Elwood City, Pennsylvania, on August 29, 1950. His father was a local carpenter, and when work in western Pennsylvania dried up in the middle 1950s, he moved the family to California.

NEW YORK YANKEES

GEORGE ZEBER — 2nd BASE

SEASONS WITH YANKEES: 1977-78

Best Season with Yankees: 1977

Games: 25 • **Batting Average: .323** • At-Bats: 65 • **Hits: 21** • Runs: 8 • **Home Runs: 3** • RBI: 10

"Shortly after we got there, when I was five years old, my father died. My mother remarried a man named Morris Davis who was really my father. He was a wonderful person, got me into baseball and took care of the family. He was an electrical engineer. He always had plenty of work," Zeber said.

Zeber graduated from Santa Ana Loara High School, was signed by the Yankees and was sent to Johnson City, Texas.

In 1970 his professional baseball career was interrupted by Army service including a year's duty in the jungles of South Vietnam.

"That not only impacted on my career, it impacted on me. It was quite a while before I could pick up my life and get my head straight after serving in Vietnam," he said.

He returned to full-time baseball duty in 1972 and was playing for Syracuse, just a stop away from Yankee Stadium, in 1973. His career derailed again when he tore up his right knee.

"It was a severe injury, and the rehab took quite a while. It wasn't until 1975 or 1976 that I really could move normally. It never was quite the same. I don't know if my career would have been longer and better if I didn't get hurt," he said.

Zeber made the Yankees out of spring training in 1977 and became close friends with the other infielders on the club—Dent, Randolph, Fred Stanley, outfielder Lou Piniella and catcher Thurman Munson.

"I had been in spring training for several years and I had played with most of the guys on the team so I really didn't have any trouble adjusting to the Yankees," he said.

Zeber was a very effective utility man playing second base, shortstop, third base and even having a couple of turns as the DH in Martin's rotating lineup. Zeber batted .323 in 25 games with three home runs.

He struck out twice in his two Series at-bats against the Dodgers but walked off with a World Series ring for his contributions to the first Yankee Series triumph in 15 years.

"That winter I met with Al Rosen, the general manager, and we argued over my 1978 contract. In those days there were no long-term deals, and I thought my strong 1977 season earned me a good raise. I was making in the 20s after a long time in pro ball and I wanted a $35,000 contract."

Rosen didn't see it that way. He pointed out that Zeber was a backup player, not a star, and unlikely to receive the kind of salary the big name players were making.

"Don't you know that garbage men in New York make $35,000 a year?" Zeber shouted across the desk to Rosen.

"Yeah, I know it," Rosen replied calmly. "Do you want to start bagging it?"

The take-it-or-leave-it attitude prevalent in those days around ball clubs between the GMs and the players forced Zeber to accept a small raise to $30,000 with the recognition that his career was not going on much longer.

Zeber failed to make the Yankees in the 1978 season, was assigned to Tacoma and came back to the Yankees for three games before being sent back to the minors again.

"I had gotten my free agency after that season and I talked to a couple of other clubs. Nothing worked out so I decided to give it up," he said.

At the age of 28, Zeber moved back home to Santa Ana, entered the real estate business and began his post-baseball life.

"I was always preparing for my baseball retirement," he said.

"I took real estate courses while I was still playing and I worked for a few firms. When it ended on the field I was ready to move ahead."

He spent several years in real estate before opening up his own home building company in the Santa Ana area. He works with investment people, does his own design and has been quite successful in building new homes.

Zeber has two children: Ryan, 25, who played some professional baseball and a daughter, Lindsay, 22, who just entered law school. He and his second wife, Terry, live in Santa Ana.

"I had some heart problems a few years back, but they fixed me up with surgery and I now feel pretty good. I put in a full day's work and enjoy almost everything I do," he said.

Zeber recognizes that he didn't make a big impact with the Yankees but he does have that 1977 World Series ring as a great memory.

"I have no regrets. When it became time to quit I realized I would have a better career outside of baseball," he said. "That's just how it worked out."

STAN
WILLIAMS

S tan Williams of the Los Angeles Dodgers gave up a couple of walks in the 1962 playoffs for the pennant against the San Francisco Giants that led to the San Francisco victory.

The Dodgers closed their clubhouse to the press after the game as so many players bawled over the defeat. Don't believe Tom Hanks. There *is* crying in baseball.

One Dodger, Duke Snider, emerged from the disaster to meet with the press. Snider had also played for the 1951 Dodgers, losers to the Giants in New York on Bobby Thomson's homer off Ralph Branca in that playoff.

"I remember my wife, Bev, consoling me after the 1951 loss by saying that at least I could be certain it would never happen again," Snider said outside the Dodger clubhouse that 1962 day. "She was wrong."

Snider survived the two Dodger playoff losses and moved on to a Hall of Fame induction.

Williams survived as well. He won 109 games in a solid 14-year career with the Dodgers, Yankees, Indians, Twins, Cardinals and Red Sox.

"I'm pretty fortunate about my baseball career," said Williams in 2003 as he drove from the Washington airport to Baltimore as part

SEASONS WITH YANKEES: 1963-64

Best Season with Yankees: 1963

Games: 29 • **Record: 9-8** • ERA: 3.21 • **Innings Pitched: 146** •
Hits Allowed: 137 • **Strikeouts: 98** • Walks: 57

of his duties as the advance scout for the Seattle Mariners, maybe baseball's toughest job.

Except for a couple of years as a stockbroker after his pitching career ended after the 1972 season, Williams has been drawing baseball checks for more than half a century.

He was traded to the Yankees after the 1962 playoff loss in a big deal for Yankee star, first baseman Moose Skowron. Skowron had been an anchor of the Yankee infield for nine seasons when he was shipped west.

"The Dodgers and the Yankees are the two most significant franchises in baseball," Williams said. "I was disappointed leaving the organization I had grown up in, but going to the Yankees was pretty exciting."

Williams was 9-8 with the 1963 Yankees and made it to the World Series for the second time against his old Los Angeles Dodgers pals.

Sandy Koufax, Don Drysdale and Johnny Podres beat the Yankees in a four-game sweep that year. Williams got in for three innings of relief. He also pitched a couple of innings against the White Sox in the 1959 Series.

All in all he was connected to six World Series teams as a player, coach, or scout and is proud of those connections.

"Fifty years in the game is pretty good," Williams said. "I've been fired a few times but that's baseball. You deal with it. I've had good and bad times in the game."

Stanley Wilson Williams was born in Enfield, New Hampshire on September 14, 1936. The family soon moved to Denver where he played baseball and basketball, loved the outdoors and grew into a tall, strong athlete.

The Dodgers signed Williams out of high school in 1955, and he made it to Los Angeles in 1958 with a 9-7 mark in 27 games. The six-foot-five 230-pound, hard-throwing right-handed pitcher was looked on as the eventual successor to Don Drysdale, then approaching his peak as a future Hall of Fame pitcher.

Williams was 5-5 with the 1959 Los Angeles pennant winners and then won 14, 15 and 14 games before being traded over to the Yankees in the deal for Skowron.

He won nine games for the Yankees in 1963, but was only 1-5 the next season before being traded over to the Indians.

"The 1963 Series was the highlight of my career. I was out there with the Yankees against the Dodgers, and that was something special," he said.

Williams moved into the bullpen with the Twins in 1970 and turned in an incredible 10-1 mark with 15 saves, one of the most impressive relief marks in modern times.

At the age of 35 he lost some hop on his heater and was released by the Red Sox after the 1972 season.

"I got into the stock market as a broker but I didn't like it very much. I missed the baseball competition and I missed the camaraderie," he said.

A couple of years after the season he got a call from Dick O'Connell, the general manager of the Red Sox.

"How would you like to manage?" O'Connell asked Williams.

Williams said he knew that Boston had just hired Darrell Johnson as their skipper for 1974.

"You want me to manage the Red Sox?" he asked O'Connell.

"No, we want you to manage our club in Bristol, Connecticut," O'Connell said.

Williams accepted the $14,000 a year job and was back in baseball. In 2003 he was roaming the country for Seattle as the advance scout.

"I work two series ahead of the team," he said. "I watch the club we will be playing and then go up to my hotel room and put all the information in a computer to [send to] the office. It's a good thing I took typing in high school. I'm usually up to 2 or 3 a.m. every night after a game in my room."

He still loves being in the game, telling tales with old pals in the ballpark press rooms, working on his scouting and helping the Mariners remain one of baseball's elite teams.

Williams and his wife of 45 years, Elaine, are the parents of two children and have three grandchildren. They make their home in Lakewood, California. Williams admits he spends more time in hotel rooms than in his Lakewood home.

"I got the toughest job in baseball," he said. "There's only one thing worse. That's no job in baseball."

TOM
TRESH

He slugged 153 home runs during eight seasons playing along-side Mickey Mantle on the Yankees, batted both ways as Mantle did and eventually named one of his sons after Mickey.

The fans, the media and some of his teammates thought they had another Mantle on the Yankees when Tom Tresh showed up in 1961. Tresh never saw it that way.

"I always tried to be the best ballplayer I could be. I never tried to be another Mickey. That couldn't happen. There was only one Mickey Mantle. I never felt any pressure from that," Tresh said.

He was a handsome 22-year-old college boy when he joined the Yankees at the end of the 1961 season, one of the most dramatic in baseball history with the Mantle/Roger Maris home run chase.

Tresh's father, Mike Tresh, had been a big-league catcher with the Chicago White Sox and Cleveland Indians from 1938 to 1949. Tom Tresh remembered some of his dad's big-league days.

"We were with Dad when he was playing in Chicago, and I used to go to the ballpark and hang around the field with the other kids of the players. It was always great fun. I think that gave me an easy adjustment to big-league play," Tresh said.

Tresh joined the Yankees in one of the peak periods of their history with four pennants in a row from 1961 to 1964, two World

SEASONS WITH YANKEES: 1961-69

Best Season with Yankees: 1962 (All-Star; Rookie of the Year)

Games: 157 • **Batting Average: .286** • At-Bats: 622 (seventh in AL) • **Hits: 178 (10th in AL)** • Runs: 94 (10th in AL) • **Home Runs: 20** • RBI: 93

Series titles and losses in October to the Los Angeles Dodgers and the St. Louis Cardinals in a stirring 1964 seven-game Series.

He broke in as a shortstop and was soon converted to an outfielder. Tresh ran well, had great range, had a strong arm and proved to be an exceptional outfielder over his eight-plus years with the Yankees.

With Johnny Keane being named Yankee manager in 1965 and proving to be a big bust, the team lost its fire and dropped quickly out of contention. The Yankees actually finished in 10th place in 1966 under Keane and resurrected manager Ralph Houk.

Tresh batted only .233 that year but hit 27 home runs as just about the only offensive threat the Yankees could present.

"The early years with the Yankees were great, but the last few years were very tough. I had some knee problems and couldn't swing or run normally," he said. "I knew the end was coming."

In 1969 Tresh was traded to Detroit for journeyman outfielder Ron Woods. He finished out the season on his bad knee but a second knee operation convinced him that his playing days were over.

Thomas Michael Tresh was born in Detroit on September 20, 1937. He played ball as a youngster at Comiskey Park with his father and in the area near the family home in Mount Pleasant.

He was signed by the Yankees out of college at Central Michigan University and joined the club in 1961. He batted .245 in nine seasons with the Yankees and Tigers, hit .277 in three World Series and collected 530 RBIs.

"Mark Belanger hit a ball that I chased down and when I pivoted to throw the knee just gave out," Tresh recalled. "I was just never the same after that."

He went to spring training with the Tigers in 1970 but soon realized he couldn't play any longer.

"I had a family to take care of and I couldn't put this pressure on them about making the team or going to the minors. I decided to go home and go into business," he said.

Tresh and his wife, Sandi, have seven children and 13 grandchildren. They make their homes in Mount Pleasant, Michigan and Venice, Florida.

After retiring from baseball, Tresh bought a struggling Kentucky Fried Chicken franchise in nearby Alma, Michigan.

"I did everything there—cooked, cleaned, hired people, opened, closed the place, put in a long workday every day," he said. "But I turned it around, and we made some money when we sold the franchise."

Tresh then returned to his alma mater at Central Michigan and worked in the alumni office and the placement office of the college for many years.

He later became first assistant baseball coach but never really was interested in being the head coach.

"It was one of those jobs where I could help the kids and do a little recruiting, but it left me with time to travel to card shows, come back for baseball events and enjoy some free time," he said.

The kids in school often asked Tresh about his Yankee days, about playing with Mickey Mantle and about his World Series appearances.

"There's no question that playing for the Yankees gave me identification in later life that really helped me in a lot of ways," he said.

Tresh often attends the Yankee Fantasy Camps where successful businessmen pay thousands of dollars for a week of vacation and baseball with former big-leaguers.

At one final camp banquet he pointed out that a ballplayer who makes the big leagues even for a day has to be a great baseball player considering the competition along the way.

"I might have had a better career if I didn't hurt my knee," he said, "but I have no regrets. It was just short of 10 years, and that is pretty good."

Tresh is also very proud of his Yankee connection.

"Sometimes I think I should just sign my name, 'Tom Tresh, New York Yankee.' That's my identification," he said.

LEN
BOEHMER

H e didn't even play on the most exciting day he ever experienced on a baseball field, yet years later Len Boehmer can still recall his emotions on June 8, 1969.

"I grew up in Flint Hill, Missouri, a town of about a hundred people, and I still live there," said Boehmer. "My father, Urban Boehmer, was one of the best amateur baseball players around here. I played ball when I was about five or six years old. I guess you could say we were really a baseball community."

Even though he lived only 45 miles from St. Louis and loved the Cardinals, Boehmer was fascinated by the Yankees and was thrilled to see Mickey Mantle almost every Saturday afternoon on television's *Game of the Week.*

"I was just an incredible Mickey Mantle fan. I followed his career and collected his baseball cards and read everything I could get my hands on about Mickey," he said.

In 1968 Boehmer went to spring training with the Yankees in Fort Lauderdale and got to meet Mantle. He was just one of the crowd trying to make the Yankees so he didn't have a chance to chat with Mantle, whose locker was at the opposite side of the room from the rookies.

SEASONS WITH YANKEES: 1969; 1971

Best Season with Yankees: 1969

Games: 45 • **Batting Average: .176** • At-Bats: 108 • **Hits: 19** •
Runs: 5 • **Home Runs: 0** • RBI: 7

Then came that June day in 1969 when all of the baseball world turned its attention to Mantle. The Yankees decided to retire Mantle's uniform No. 7 in an incredibly touching ceremony.

All of the Yankees were on the field, and all of the celebrities collected by the Yankees were on hand to congratulate Mantle for his brilliant Yankee career.

"I just got so emotional when they handed him his uniform shirt and that plaque that they would put up on the wall at Yankee Stadium. I was so moved by Mantle's speech thanking the Yankees and thanking the fans. It was a day I will never forget," he said.

Leonard Joseph Stephen Boehmer was born in Flint Hill, Missouri, on June 28, 1941. He knew he wanted to be a baseball player almost from the time he could reason.

He grew to be a tall, handsome infielder who starred on the baseball team at St. Louis University. After his sophomore year at St. Louis, two clubs—the New York Yankees and the Cincinnati Reds—showed interest in him.

"I looked at those two teams and figured my chances were better for a big-league career with the Reds than the Yankees. I was a shortstop back then. Tony Kubek was the Yankee shortstop in 1961, and I knew he would be around for a long while. Cincinnati was always looking for a shortstop."

The Reds gave Boehmer an $18,000 bonus and sent him to the minor leagues. He had several good seasons, fielded well and joined the Cincinnati club for a couple of games at the end of the 1967 season.

The Yankees obtained Boehmer after that season in a deal for pitcher Bill Henry.

"I was really happy about that. I was with the Yankees, and Kubek had retired by that time. I thought I had a good chance to make the club as the starting shortstop," he said.

He had a strong minor league season in 1968 and made it to the Yankees as a backup infielder in 1969. He hit only .176 in 45 games and that was about the end of his Yankee dreams. He was back in the minors in 1970 and was called up for three more games in 1971.

It wasn't long before he came home to Missouri and entered his father's plumbing supply business.

"My grandfather had built the building, and my father and his brother started the business about 40 years ago. Then my brother and I ran it for a lot of years. I just recently retired, and we turned it over to my two sons, Stephen and Robert," he said.

Boehmer didn't make a great impact in his baseball career, but the third generation of brothers running the plumbing supply business in Flint Hill certainly is significant for that industry.

Boehmer said that even though his baseball career was short and rather uneventful, he still gets attention around home for having been a member of the New York Yankees.

"I got a lot of baseball pictures on the wall and a lot of gloves and bats that I brought back home. I also have a huge afghan with the Yankee *NY* logo in the middle of it. Everybody enjoys that," he said.

Boehmer and his wife, Alice, have four children and eight grandchildren. Most of them live in the area so he enjoys frequent visits from family members.

"I play golf two or three times a week and I watch the games on television. I haven't been back to Yankee Stadium since I stopped playing but the Yankees are still my favorite team," he said.

Boehmer said he was interested in seeing how his retirement goes. He promised his sons he would stay out of their way in the business.

"Maybe I'll take a trip to New York and visit the new Yankee Stadium. It must look a lot different now from when I played there," he said.

Boehmer might even visit Monument Park and catch a good close up of the tribute to his hero Mickey Mantle.

MIKE HEGAN

There has been a Hegan around big-league baseball for more than 60 years. Jim Hegan played from 1941 through 1960 and then coached. Jim's son Mike Hegan broke into the big leagues in 1964, played through 1977 and later became a broadcaster with the Milwaukee Brewers. In 2003 he was completing his 15th year as a broadcaster for his father's old team, the Cleveland Indians.

"It's been a wonderful ride," said Hegan, as he sat in a park in Minneapolis one pleasant summer afternoon before the Indians were scheduled to meet the Twins that evening. "I've barely missed a week of big-league baseball from the time I joined the Yankees out of Holy Cross."

Jim Hegan was a stylish catcher through his 17 years in the big leagues, handling such Hall of Famers as Bob Feller, Bob Lemon and Early Wynn and playing under Hall of Fame skipper Lou Boudreau.

Mike Hegan was a stylish first baseman over his 12-year playing career, which included seasons with the Yankees as a teammate to Hall of Famers Mickey Mantle, Whitey Ford, and Yogi Berra, as well as time spent with Reggie Jackson and Catfish Hunter in Oakland.

Hegan hit .242 in his 12 seasons while his dad batted only .228 in his 17 years. Each of the Hegans made it to the World Series twice.

SEASONS WITH YANKEES: 1964-67; 1973-74

Best Season with Yankees: 1973

Games: 37 (as a Yankee) • **Batting Average: .275** • At-Bats: 131 • **Hits: 36** • Runs: 12 • **Home Runs: 6** • RBI: 14

Jim Hegan played against the Braves in 1948 in a winning Series and was swept by the Giants in 1954; Mike Hegan was on the losing Yankees in 1964 and the winning A's in 1972.

James Michael Hegan was born July 21, 1942 in Cleveland, Ohio, while his father was catching for the Indians. He grew up in Cleveland, attended St. Ignatius High School and then entered Holy Cross where he starred in football and basketball.

The handsome son of the handsome catcher and coach was signed by the Yankees in 1961 for a $60,000 bonus.

"I had been playing in a summer league in Boston when the Yankees signed me. I started in the organization in 1962 and made it to the big club in 1964 for a few games. Then I spent a year in Syracuse before being called up again," he said.

After 1964 the Yankees were going through a transition with their older players—Tony Kubek, Bobby Richardson, Berra, Ford and Mantle either leaving the game or aging rapidly.

By 1967 the Yankees had decided that Mantle, weary from the baseball wars and a hard life, was unable to play in the outfield any longer. Manager Ralph Houk decided he would move Mantle to first base.

"I became his caddy, his backup," said Hegan. "Mickey would play six or seven innings, and then I would get in there on defense if we were ahead. I would usually get in anyway because it was hard for Mickey to make it for nine innings."

Hegan played in 68 games with only a .136 average but probably saved Mantle for another season. Mickey retired after 1968.

"Actually I thought Mickey would have been better off in the outfield. You only have to run straight ahead in the outfield. At first you are twisting and turning and bending and stretching, a lot tougher on your legs," he said.

In 1969 Hegan was selected by the expansion Seattle Pilots and had a fine season with the new club. He batted .292 in 95 games and achieved literary baseball immortality as one of the players on the team described wittily in Jim Bouton's iconoclastic work *Ball Four*.

The team moved to Milwaukee the next year under the ownership of present baseball commissioner Bud Selig.

"I get a lot of letters from kids wanting my autograph because I played with the Pilots. There weren't that many of us. The baseball cards are usually of me in a Yankee uniform but once in a while I get my Seattle card in the mail," he said.

Hegan was traded to Oakland in 1971 and played with the world champions in 1972. He had his best year with the bat, hitting .329 in 98 games. He was traded back to the Yankees the next year and then moved back to Milwaukee for his final four seasons in the big leagues.

"About three or four years before I quit playing I started doing some broadcasting. I knew I would get into that when it was over. I had been signed out of college, and my parents made me promise I would get a degree. They knew baseball didn't last forever. I finally earned a degree in psychology from Calvin Coolidge College in Boston," he said.

Mike and Nancy Hegan are the parents of two children and have two grandchildren who had never seen Mike in his Yankee uniform, until recently.

"The Yankees invited me back as part of the team's 100th anniversary in 2003," said Hegan. "The entire family was there, and it was something very special."

Hegan, who now makes his home in Hilton Head, South Carolina, in the off season so he can golf almost every day, is proud of his Yankee past.

"That's what people ask about—playing with the Yankees, playing in Yankee Stadium, what Mickey was like, all the Yankee talk. Some collectors still are sharp and want Seattle Pilots stuff," he said.

Jim Hegan was as smooth a catcher as there was in his big-league time, and Mike Hegan was a graceful first baseman who helped ease Mickey Mantle through his trying final days on the field.

Jim Hegan was a long-time Yankee coach who was even there in the bullpen when his son joined the team.

"Our family link to the Yankees is pretty strong," Hegan said. "It was important to me and it was very important to our grandchildren when I suited up once again as a Yankee."

JAKE
GIBBS

H e was an All-America football player at the University of Mississippi, the captain and quarterback of the 1960 Sugar Bowl winners and national champions and a candidate for an NFL job with Cleveland and Houston.

Then Jake Gibbs turned his back on the game and signed a $100,000 bonus baby contract to play baseball for the New York Yankees.

"I never looked back," said Gibbs. "I never had any regrets about choosing baseball. I knew I would have a longer career in baseball than football, and I did."

Gibbs played 10 years as a catcher with the Yankees from 1962 through 1971, had a lifetime .233 average and then stayed connected to the game through college and professional coaching and managing.

Football didn't forget about the accomplishments Gibbs recorded on the gridiron. In 1995 he was selected as a member of the College Football Hall of Fame.

After his Yankee playing career ended, Gibbs accepted a position as baseball coach and football recruiter at his alma mater in Oxford. He put in 19 seasons there before the NCAA ruled that college coaches in one sport could not participate in a second sport.

SEASONS WITH YANKEES: 1962-71

Best Season with Yankees: 1970

Games: 49 • Batting Average: .301 • At-Bats: 153 • Hits: 46 •
Runs: 23 • Home Runs: 8 • RBI: 26

"I stayed home, played golf, enjoyed the family and then got a call from the Yankees. They brought me back to New York to be the catching coach in 1992 and 1993. The next year I was the manager at their Tampa club and won a Florida State League title. Then I decided to go home for good," Gibbs said.

Jerry Dean Gibbs was born November 7, 1938 in Grenada, Mississippi.

"I don't know how I got the name of Jake," he said. "I can't remember anybody ever calling me Jerry Dean. It was just Jake as a kid and Jake from then on."

His father, Frank Gibbs, worked on the country roads in Grenada and then got into local politics. He served as a supervisor in the Grenada area for many years.

Gibbs won six letters in high school baseball and football as a shortstop and third baseman in baseball and a quarterback in football.

"I didn't do much in football in college until my senior year. I kept getting injured with a broken bone in my foot and later a broken nose. I stayed healthy in 1960, and we won everything," he said.

The Yankees had only one high salaried bonus kid up until 1960—Frank Leja. He joined the team with a $100,000 bonus in 1954. He got one big-league hit in two seasons, making the Yankees very leery of bonus players.

Gibbs was a fine prospect being chased by the football scouts as well as baseball people. The Yankees plunged in, signed him and sent the six-foot, 180-pounder to their minor league system.

"I was an infielder in those days, and then I was drafted in 1962. An Army captain said I would become a catcher. When I came back to the Yankees, Ralph Houk told me I had to become a catcher if I wanted to make the ball club. I knew I'd rather be in the big leagues so I became a catcher," Gibbs said.

Gibbs started out behind Hall of Famer Yogi Berra, who became his manager in 1964, and highly talented Elston Howard. Houk moved up to GM and saw the value in having Gibbs on the club. Houk had been a backup catcher to Berra in Yogi's younger days with an eight-year career as a backup.

Gibbs got into nine games for the 1962, 1963 and 1964 Yankee pennant winners and then caught in 21 games for the 1965 Yankees. He was the anchor catcher over the next three seasons.

He was a solid receiver but his batting skills didn't make the Yankees think he was the true successor to Berra. The Yankees would be uncomfortable with their catching situation until Thurman Munson showed up in 1969.

After his Yankee days ended, Gibbs enjoyed coaching baseball at his alma mater and appreciated the identification he always had as a longtime member of the Yankees.

"I was on the football field at a game we were playing against Alabama while I was still with the Yankees," Gibbs recalled. "There was coach [Paul] Bryant with his famous hat. He walked up to me and just whispered. 'You had a great year.' He was a big baseball fan," Gibbs said.

One other time Gibbs received a visitor from New York. It was the Yankee owner, Michael Burke, who was being honored in Gibbs's hometown. Famed Mississippi writer Willie Morris joined Burke in Gibbs's home prior to a dinner that evening to look at some Yankee pictures and talk baseball.

"They stayed all afternoon. That was quite a day listening to those guys tell stories," he said.

After he retired from managing in the Yankee system, Gibbs returned home to play a lot of golf, enjoy dinners with his family and listen to country music.

He and his wife of 41 years, Patricia, have three sons and six grandchildren, all of whom live within easy driving distance of the Gibbs home in Oxford.

"People like to talk about my Yankee days and look at those pictures of me and Mickey [Mantle] and me and Whitey [Ford] and all the guys on those teams. They were wonderful days, and I enjoyed every minute I spent with the Yankees in New York," he said.

Gibbs was never the catcher the Yankees imagined when they signed him for that big bonus, but he gave the team a lot of loyalty and dedication over the years.

He certainly turned out to be the most popular Yankee in Oxford, Mississippi.

RYNE DUREN

He would bound out of the Yankee bullpen over that small out-field fence in deep left field, hold a warm up jacket over his right arm, fling it to the batboy near the mound and take the baseball from Yankee manager Casey Stengel.

This was in 1958 or 1959 when Ryne Duren was king of the hill. He was the hardest throwing relief pitcher in baseball who could get the ball up to the plate at 100 miles an hour or more.

The routine was always the same.

Duren would stretch on the first warm-up pitch, stare down at the catcher and then fire a baseball near home plate. The ball would be 10 feet over the head of the catcher, crashing down against the wire mesh fence behind home plate, protecting the seated fans from foul balls.

"It was just a gimmick," Duren said years later. "The idea was to excite the fans and scare the hitters."

The gimmick became Duren's calling card, his identification as the mean man of the mound and one of the most successful relief pitchers in the eras when relief pitchers were just becoming impor-tant members of the team.

ryne duren

YANKEES   PiTCHER

SEASONS WITH YANKEES: 1958-61

Best Season with Yankees: 1958 (All-Star)

Games: 44 (ninth in AL) • **Record: 6-4** • ERA: 2.02 • **Saves: 20 (first in AL)** • Innings Pitched: 75 $^2/_3$ • **Hits Allowed: 40** • Strikeouts: 87 • **Walks: 43**

Prior to the 1950s, relief pitchers were usually old starters with poor arms or young pitchers without speed. The starters were supposed to go nine innings in those days. Relief pitchers might not get into more than 15 or 20 games a season.

In 2001, Yankee relief ace Mariano Rivera pitched in 71 games and led the team in career saves with 243 going into the 2003 season at age 33.

Duren led the American League with 20 saves in 1958 after coming over to the Yankees the previous June in a famous trade involving Yankee bad boy Billy Martin.

He had 14 saves the following season and nine for the 1960 Yankees.

"I don't remember too many of them," Duren said in 2003. "All of those years were just a big haze."

Duren is a recovering alcoholic and admits to drinking heavily before, sometimes during and certainly after most of his wins and saves in his Yankee career.

In 1968, after his playing days ended, his life almost ended as well after several suicide attempts. He made it through an Alcohol Anonymous session, then another and another until he could soon claim sobriety for a year, then 10 years, and now in 2003 to 35 years of sobriety.

"It's all a challenge," he said one day as he visited New York for teammate Whitey Ford's 75th birthday party. "Not a day goes by that I don't want a drink."

A waiter walked up to Ford and Duren as they talked in a hotel ballroom before the dinner event. Ford ordered a beer. Duren smiled, said "Me too" and then settled for a soft drink.

"It's the culture," he said. "People drink, especially ballplayers and former ballplayers. It's hard not to be pushed into it."

Duren's life and career, especially these battles with booze, were chronicled warmly and wonderfully in a new book entitled, *I Can See Clearly Now*, a detailed examination of the long, hard journey Duren has pursued during his life.

Rinold George Duren Jr. was born in the farming community of Cazenovia, Wisconsin on February 22, 1929.

"There were a lot of town teams around there when I was a kid, and we used to travel in the summer from town to town playing in those games. I played every position as a kid, but I always enjoyed pitching most," he said.

Duren grew to be a husky six-foot-two lad weighing more than 190 pounds with a strong right arm and terrible nearsightedness.

"I wore glasses as far back as I can remember. They just kept getting thicker and thicker as I got older," he said. "When I went to the big leagues we played mostly day games and the sun bothered me. I always wore dark, tinted glasses," he said.

He was signed by the old St. Louis Browns. They moved to Baltimore after owner Bill Veeck sold out in a sad baseball loss. Duren pitched one game for the Orioles at the end of the 1954 season.

He spent the next two years in the minors and was traded to Kansas City after the 1956 season. He had an 0-3 mark but had 37 strikeouts in 42 innings, a ratio that impressed Yankee GM George Weiss.

When Weiss decided to unload Martin after the famed Copacabana nightclub furor (and because he had a young second baseman named Bobby Richardson ready to take over the position), he insisted that Duren be part of the deal.

"The Yankees were a hard drinking lot so I fit right in," said Duren.

Mickey Mantle, Ford, Hank Bauer and several other teammates were party boys as Duren tagged along and outdid them all in post-game drink-a-thons.

"That's what we did—play ball, win and celebrate by drinking," he said.

One of Duren's parties got him in trouble. After the Yankees defeated Milwaukee in the 1958 World Series with a rousing come back after a 3-1 deficit, the train ride back to New York was rather raucous.

Duren came up to backup catcher Ralph Houk, a World War II combat Ranger and later Yankee manager and GM, who was quietly puffing a victory cigar.

Duren squashed the cigar in Houk's mouth. Houk reacted as any former Ranger would. He decked Duren.

The rumpus was witnessed by *New York Post* sportswriter Leonard Shecter, later the editor of Jim Bouton's iconoclastic *Ball Four*. Shecter wrote a front-page story for his tabloid newspaper.

It cost Duren money in fines. It also set his image as a drinker and carouser.

Duren moved on to the expansion Los Angeles Angels in 1961 and later pitched for Philadelphia, Cincinnati and Washington. His career mark was 27-44 with 57 saves and a 3.83 ERA after 10 seasons.

He took on some odd jobs after he left baseball, drinking even more heavily as he grew depressed about missing the game. He came close to death several times and finally, with the help of family and friends, made it through AA programs.

He has spent the last 35 years of his life writing, lecturing and consulting with people and agencies on the evils of alcohol.

Duren and his wife Diane are the parents of four children and have seven grandchildren. They live in Middleton, Wisconsin and Venice, Florida.

"If I didn't find AA I wouldn't be here now," Duren said in 2003. "I think God just sent me down to help others fight this addiction."

Where Have You Gone?

RICK CERONE

Thurman Munson crashed his $1.5 million Cessna Citation twin engine jet a thousand feet short of the Canton-Akron Airport in Ohio on August 2, 1979. The plane sliced into some trees, flew past Greensburg Road, crashed into the ground below a rise that led to the runway and quickly caught fire.

Munson, 32 years old, the captain and catcher of the Yankees, was found dead in the pilot's seat from smoke and fire.

The Yankees flew to Munson's funeral in Canton a week later for an emotional farewell to their team leader.

All of baseball was stunned at the tragic loss of this fine ballplayer at such an early age and in such a sad way.

Jerry Narron was the backup catcher for the Yankees. He was not able to handle the position on a full-time basis. So, the Yankees quickly began searching for a catcher.

As they studied rosters and discussed the big-league catching situation around baseball, one name was mentioned most often as a possible successor to Munson.

On November 1, 1979, barely three months after Munson's death, the Yankees made a deal with Toronto that sent 1976 home run hero Chris Chambliss to the Blue Jays for catcher Rick Cerone.

SEASONS WITH YANKEES: 1980-84;
1987; 1990-91

Best Season with Yankees: 1980 (seventh in MVP voting)

Games: 147 • **Batting Average: .277** • At-Bats: 519 • **Hits: 144** •
Runs: 70 • **Doubles: 30** • Home Runs: 14 • **RBI: 85**

They were bringing the New Jersey kid home.

Richard Aldo Cerone was born in Newark, New Jersey on May 19, 1954. He starred at Essex Catholic High School and won a scholarship to nearby Seton Hall University. He was an Academic All American in 1975 as well as the catching star of the Seton Hall team that competed with the best college players in the country in the College World Series.

He was a first-round draft choice of the Cleveland Indians after graduating in 1975 and got into 14 games for the Indians in 1975 and 1976 before being traded to Toronto.

He became the Blue Jays' top receiver a couple of years later and seemed on his way to a long and successful career with Toronto.

Then came the Munson crash.

"I had mixed emotions when I was traded from Toronto. I had gotten comfortable there with a young club and knew I had a bright future. But of course playing for the Yankees was exciting, and I was coming back home where I had grown up," he said.

While all eyes of his teammates, fans and press were on him, Cerone made a comfortable adjustment to the Yankees' catching job. He was a tough out, batted .277 with 85 RBIs in 1980, was a smooth receiver and soon gained the respect—as Munson had before him—of the Yankee pitchers.

He made it to the World Series with the Yankees in 1981 and was soon considered one of the leaders of George Steinbrenner's team.

As the Yankees slumped badly over the next few years, the outspoken Cerone was often quoted in the local press complaining about Steinbrenner's interference on the field.

On one occasion Steinbrenner came into the Yankee clubhouse—an almost unexpected event—and berated the team for not playing hard.

In a stage whisper overheard by most of his teammates, Cerone told the Yankee owner where he thought he should go. Most players laughed and the meeting ended.

Steinbrenner and Cerone later made up, with the owner understanding that his catcher was a battler and a competitor, much like the late catcher of the Yankees.

"We both got over it," Cerone later said. "George knew it was said in the heat of battle."

Cerone was later traded to Atlanta, came back to the Yankees twice and also played for Milwaukee, Boston and Montreal in a solid 18-year big-league career. His lifetime mark was .245, but he always was considered a fine receiver.

Cerone followed his catching career by broadcasting baseball with the Yankees and other clubs and also bought into ownership with the Wilmington (North Carolina) Blue Rocks.

In 1999 Cerone created the Newark Bears in the independent Atlantic League and was instrumental in the building of the beautiful new Riverfront Stadium in Newark, the successor to the old Newark Bears Stadium once owned by the Yankees.

The team won the league crown in 2002, and Cerone was recognized as one of New Jersey's most distinguished citizens along with musical icon Bruce Springsteen.

Cerone and his three daughters reside in Teaneck. The former Yankee catcher is active in dozens of New Jersey charities, still shows up at Yankee Stadium for special events and is proud of the success of his Newark team.

"Playing was fun, but owning your own team is even more fun," Cerone said. "The best position in baseball is being the boss."

PETE WARD

In the late 1960s to save a few bucks on hot summer nights, Pete Ward lived in a tent on the outfield grass in the low minor leagues of Texas.

Phil Linz, a star in the league and later an opponent with the Yankees against Ward's White Sox, never let Ward forget it—even when both were making a living as big-league infielders in the 1960s.

"There's Petey Ward. He used to live in a tent," Linz would howl from the Yankee bench when Ward took the field with the White Sox.

Ward laughs at the memories of those days more than 45 years ago as he sits in the living room of his glamorous home outside of Portland, Oregon.

"I only got $4,000 to sign," said Ward. "It didn't go very far."

Ward spent nine years in the big leagues with Baltimore, the White Sox and finally the Yankees during the 1970 season. He batted .260 in six games for the Yankees and was released the following spring at the age of 31. His career mark was .254 in nine seasons.

"I did some managing, coaching and scouting in the Yankee organization after that," he said. "I feel very much a part of the Yankees. I was with the organization as a scout and a minor league man-

NEW YORK YANKEES

PETE
WARD   1st BASE

SEASONS WITH YANKEES: 1970

Best Season with Yankees: 1970

Games: 66 • **Batting Average: .260** • At-Bats: 77 • **Hits: 20** • Runs: 5 • **Home Runs: 1** • RBI: 18

ager in 1977 and 1978. George Steinbrenner gave us World Series rings, so that makes me a Yankee."

Ward, a smooth-fielding third baseman who played some outfield and some third base, played on several good Chicago teams that challenged the Yankees.

"We were ahead of the Yankees in 1964 when they came to Comiskey Park. We swept them in a four-game Series. That's when Linz played the harmonica on the bus and everything changed for them," Ward said.

Peter Thomas Ward was born July 26, 1939 in Montreal, Quebec, Canada. His father was a noted hockey player and coach and moved the family to Portland for a hockey coaching job when Pete was eight years old.

His older brother played hockey, but Pete became more interested in the local game, baseball, and won a baseball scholarship to Lewis and Clark College in Portland.

He was signed by the Orioles in 1958 and after some time in his Texas tent, he made it to the big leagues with Baltimore in 1962.

Baltimore traded Ward along with future Hall of Famer Hoyt Wilhelm to Chicago for future Hall of Fame shortstop Luis Aparicio after the 1962 season.

"Being in a deal with two Hall of Famers was pretty impressive," he said.

He put in half a dozen seasons as a solid left-handed hitter with good power and a sure glove for the White Sox before moving over to the Yankees.

"I was pretty excited about that," he said. "The Yankees were down in those days, but they still had that reputation and that glory from the past. I was pretty emotional when I walked on the Stadium grass for the first time wearing those pinstripes."

He had but one quick season as a Yankee player but got into the organization as a coach, scout and manager through the 1970s.

Ward, his wife, Margaret, and their three sons settled in Portland and Ward soon was putting in some winter time at a travel agency.

He was very active in local charity events and sponsored an annual dinner in Portland. Some of the biggest names in the game—from Mickey Mantle and Whitey Ford to Willie Mays and Mike Schmidt—helped him raise money for local causes.

"I bought the business a few years back with a partner and now we have about 40 employees. We book tours all over. People love to go to ballparks around the country through our tours," Ward said.

Ward said he is constantly running into former teammates and opponents as he travels across the country with his agency's tour groups.

"We all love to get together and just reminisce about the old days. I am very happy doing what I'm doing now, but it sure was fun playing in the big leagues," he said.

Ward said his Yankee memories in a down season were not significant, but he has one story of a game he loves to tell old friends and teammates.

"They had this game in Yankee Stadium between the Mets and Yankees that was a big summer attraction before they had inter-league play. It was called the Mayor's Trophy Game. I was playing against the Mets and I was facing a young hard thrower by the name of Nolan Ryan. He had made a big splash in the World Series the year before in 1969 so I knew who he was. Everybody said he could just blow the ball by you. I faced him once with two guys on, and I hit a three-run home run. That's a great Yankee memory for me," he said.

Ward said he often wears his Yankee World Series ring when he is making a pitch for a big travel deal. His customers are usually pretty impressed.

"They all start talking baseball and talking about the Yankees, and before you know it I have closed a nice deal for a large group trip," he said. "The Yankees have certainly helped my career."

Ward said he still stayed up with baseball for both business reasons and pleasure.

"Once you wear that big-league uniform you never really get away from it," he said. "I go to a few games while I am on these tours and I see a lot of minor league baseball around this area."

The guy who once saved a few bucks by sleeping in a tent in a Texas ballpark now has plenty of room in his Portland home for his children and five grandchildren who live in the area.

"If Linz ever gets out this way I can even put him up," laughed Ward.

"We would have a few tales of the old days to exchange."

TOMMY HENRICH

A strikeout in the fourth game of the 1941 World Series and a leadoff homer in the ninth inning of the first game of the 1949 World Series, both against the Brooklyn Dodgers, immortalized Tommy Henrich for Yankee fans.

The guy they called "Old Reliable" for his clutch hitting—an accurate nickname put on him by broadcaster Russ Hodges—is still alert and active at the age of 90 despite a couple of strokes and some other illnesses.

"I'm better than I sound," Henrich said over the phone in the summer of 2003.

Henrich had to turn down an invitation to throw out the first ball at the Yankees 2003 Old Timers Game because it was a little too much to travel from his home in Monterey, California. He now lives near a daughter with his wife of 62 years, Eileen. They have five children and six grandchildren.

Henrich played 11 years with a lifetime .282 average after being declared a free agent because he was signed out of high school illegally. The Yankees gave him $20,000, the largest bonus they had ever offered up until that time.

He was on seven World Series winners, but two Series games made his reputation.

TOMMY "OLD RELIABLE" HENRICH
OUTFIELD

SEASONS WITH YANKEES: 1937-50

Best Season with Yankees: 1948 (All-Star; sixth in MVP voting)

Games: 146 • Batting Average: .308 • At-Bats: 588 • Hits: 181 (eighth in AL) • Runs: 138 (first in AL) • Doubles: 42 (second in AL) • Triples: 14 (first in AL) • Home Runs: 25 (sixth in AL) • RBI: 100 (10th in AL) • Slugging Percentage: .554 (third in AL) • Total Bases: 326 (second in AL) • Walks: 76 • Strikeouts: 42

The Dodgers led the Yankees 4-3 in the top of the ninth in Brooklyn in the fourth game of the 1941 October Classic. There were two out. One more out would even the Series at 2-2. Brooklyn reliever Hugh Casey got two strikes on Henrich and then unleashed a wicked breaking ball. Legend has it that it was an illegal spitball.

"I can't say," Henrich later said, "but it sure broke a long way."

He swung and missed it. So did Dodger catcher Mickey Owen. Henrich ran to first base, and the Yankees rallied behind the muff for four runs and a 7-3 win.

In 1949, Don Newcombe, the big, hard thrower of the Dodgers, and Allie Reynolds, the right-handed power pitcher of the Yankees, matched up in a fantastic battle. The game was scoreless into the bottom of the ninth. Newcombe threw a fastball, and Henrich deposited it into the lower right field seats as the Yankees won 1-0 on their way to a 4-1 Series win.

"Those two games are the ones most people ask me about," Henrich said.

Thomas David Henrich was born February 20, 1913, in Massillon, Ohio. After an exceptional high school career as a baseball and football player, he was signed by the Tigers. The original signing was ruled illegal by commissioner Kenesaw Mountain Landis because of Henrich's age and class. As a free agent, he then was courted by several clubs and chose the Yankees.

Babe Ruth was gone, but he had been a boyhood hero of Henrich's.

"I fell in love with Babe Ruth. Every kid in my time fell in love with him and those home runs," Henrich said.

Henrich later met Ruth as the Sultan of Swat was doing a radio show and interviewed the newest Yankee. He asked Henrich if he had cashed his bonus check. Henrich told the Babe he hadn't cashed it yet.

"Go ahead and cash it," Ruth advised him. "If it is signed by the boss [Yankee owner Jacob Ruppert] it won't bounce."

Joe DiMaggio was in his second season with the Yankees and Lou Gehrig was having his last great year as a Yankee in 1937 before illness set him down.

"I liked the way DiMaggio played. He was all business, a pro, you know. Not the friendliest guy in the world. You know what? I played with him for a lot of years and he was making big money. He never took me to dinner," Henrich said.

He was closer to Gehrig and visited with the team captain in 1941 shortly before he died at his New York home.

One of Henrich's great memories was DiMaggio's 56-game hitting streak in 1941.

"He was up to about 30 or 35 games and people were starting to notice," Henrich recalled. "We were playing in Washington, and some kid reached into the dugout and stole Joe's bat. Now you know how superstitious guys are about their bats. Well, it was a day or two before Joe got it back. I think some of his Italian friends put out the word that if the bat didn't show up, they would be in serious trouble."

DiMaggio got his bat back and continued hitting through 56 games. Then he was stopped in Cleveland.

"When we got to Washington a few days later we decided to give him a party. A few of us went out and bought this silver tray, and all the guys autographed it for Joe. Lefty Gomez, who was Joe's pal, brought him to the room as a surprise. I played the piano and everybody sang, 'He's a jolly good fellow,' Joe was pretty touched, especially for him," said Henrich.

Henrich hit .272 in his final year with the Yankees at age 37. He was released after that season but brought back to spring training in 1951 to work with a kid named Mickey Mantle.

"I had never seen anything like that. Both sides of the plate. And such power. He was something. He could hit but he couldn't catch a fly ball. I got out early with him, and pretty soon that great speed helped him become a fine outfielder," Henrich said.

Henrich went home the following season. He joined a manufacturing company around his home in Canton, Ohio, served as a sales representative for many years, played a lot of golf and showed up often at Yankee Stadium for Old Timers Games and special baseball events.

Henrich never lost his sense of humor or his joyful countenance. In his 90s, he kidded about a birthday card he received from teammate Yogi Berra on his 90th birthday.

"He put in there, 'Remember Tom, it ain't over 'til it's over.' That was Yogi," he said.

In 2003, as he skipped the reunion of some of his teammates at the Stadium, Henrich was asked if he was proud to be one of the oldest living Yankees. That drew a hearty laugh from Old Reliable.

"I'm proud to be *alive*," said Henrich.

Also By Maury Allen

All Roads Lead to October

China Spy

Jackie Robinson: A Life Remembered

Memories of the Mick

After the Miracle

Roger Maris: A Man for All Seasons

Sweet Lou (With Lou Piniella)

Mr. October: The Reggie Jackson Story

Damn Yankee: The Billy Martin Story

You Could Look It Up

Where Have You Gone, Joe DiMaggio?

Big-Time Baseball

Baseball: The Lives Behind The Seams

Bo: Pitching and Wooing

Voices Of Sport

Now Wait A Minute, Casey

The Record Breakers

The Incredible Mets

Joe Namath's Sportin' Life

Reprieve From Hell

Ten Great Moments In Sports

Reggie Jackson: The Three Million Dollar Man

Ron Guidry: Louisiana Lightning

Jim Rice: Power Hitter

Greatest Pro Quarterbacks

Baseball's 100